I0670986

BROTHERS
OF PITY

AND OTHER TALES OF BEASTS AND MEN

JULIANA HORATIA EWING

1st WORLD
LIBRARY
Literary Society

Brothers of Pity and Other Tales of Beasts and Men

Juliana Horatia Ewing

© 1st World Library, 2009
PO Box 2211
Fairfield, IA 52556
www.1stworldlibrary.com
First Edition

LCCN: 2009923468

Softcover ISBN: 978-1-4218-8857-6
Hardcover ISBN: 978-1-4218-8956-6
eBook ISBN: 978-1-4218-8758-6

Purchase *"Brothers of Pity and Other Tales of Beasts and Men"*
as a traditional bound book at:
www.1stWorldLibrary.com/purchase.asp?ISBN=978-1-4218-8857-6

1st World Library is a literary, educational organization
dedicated to:

- Creating a free internet library of downloadable ebooks

- Hosting writing competitions and offering book publishing
  scholarships.

Interested in more 1st World Library books? contact:
literacy@1stworldlibrary.com
Check us out at: www.1stworldlibrary.com

1ˢᵗ World Library Literary Society

Giving Back to the World

"If you want to work on the core problem, it's early school literacy."

- **James Barksdale, former CEO of Netscape**

"No skill is more crucial to the future of a child, or to a democratic and prosperous society, than literacy."

- **Los Angeles Times**

"Literacy... means far more than learning how to read and write... The aim is to transmit... knowledge and promote social participation."

- **UNESCO**

"Literacy is not a luxury, it is a right and a responsibility. If our world is to meet the challenges of the twenty-first century we must harness the energy and creativity of all our citizens."

- **President Bill Clinton**

"Parents should be encouraged to read to their children, and teachers should be equipped with all available techniques for teaching literacy, so the varying needs and capacities of individual kids can be taken into account."

- **Hugh Mackay**

DEDICATED

TO MY DEAR SISTER

HORATIA KATHARINE FRANCES GATTY.

J.H.E.

PREFACE TO FIRST EDITION

These tales have appeared, during some years past, in *Aunt Judy's Magazine for Young People*.

"Father Hedgehog and his Neighbours," and "Toots and Boots," were both suggested by Fedor Flinzer's clever pictures; but "Toots" was also "a real person." In his latter days he was an honorary member of the Royal Engineers' Mess at Aldershot, and, on occasion, dined at table.

"The Hens of Hencastle" is not mine. It is a free translation from the German of Victor Bluethgen, by Major Yeatman-Biggs, R.A., to whom I am indebted for permission to include it in my volume, as a necessary prelude to "Flaps." The story took my fancy greatly, but the ending seemed to me imperfect and unsatisfactory, especially in reference to so charming a character as the old watch dog, and I wrote "Flaps" as a sequel.

The frontispiece was designed specially for this volume, by Mr. Charles Whymper, and the *Fratello della Misericordia* (from a photograph kindly sent me by a friend) is by the same artist.

J.H.E.

PREFACE TO NEW EDITION

The foregoing Preface was written by Mrs. Ewing for the first edition of *Brothers of Pity, and Other Tales.* The book contains five stories, illustrated by the pictures of which my sister speaks; and it is still sold by the S.P.C.K. "Toots and Boots" was so minutely adapted to Flinzer's pictures, that the tale suffers in being parted from them. Still, it is to be hoped that readers of the un-illustrated version will not have as much difficulty as Toots in solving the mystery of the Mouse's escape! I have added four more tales of "Beasts and Men" to the present edition, as they have not been included in any previous collections of my sister's stories. "A Week Spent in a Glass Pond" appeared first in *Aunt Judy's Magazine*, October 1876, and was afterwards published separately with coloured illustrations. The habits of the water beasts are described with the strictest fidelity to nature, even the delicate differences in character between the Great and the Big Black water beetles are most accurately drawn.

"Among the Merrows" has not been republished since it came out in *Aunt Judy's Magazine*, November 1872. At that time the Crystal Palace Aquarium was a novelty, and the Zoological Station at Naples not fully formed—but, though the paper is behind the times in statistics, it is worth retaining for other reasons.

"Tiny's Tricks and Toby's Tricks" as a specimen of

versification might perhaps have been included in the volume of *Verses for Children*, but it seemed best to keep it with the "Owl Hoots," as these papers were the last that Mrs. Ewing wrote. The first appeared in *The Child's Pictorial Magazine* a few days before her death, and the "Hoots" soon afterwards. The illustrations to both were drawn by Mr. Gordon Browne at my sister's special request, and they are now reproduced with gratitude for his labour of love.

HORATIA K. F. EDEN.

October 1895.

CONTENTS

BROTHERS OF PITY 11

FATHER HEDGEHOG AND HIS NEIGHBOURS 28

TOOTS AND BOOTS 81

THE HENS OF HENCASTLE 104

FLAPS...123

A WEEK SPENT IN A GLASS POND...............................135

AMONG THE MERROWS..146

TINY'S TRICKS AND TOBY'S TRICKS...........................165

THE OWL IN THE IVY BUSH 172

BROTHERS OF PITY

"Who dug his grave?"

* * * * *

"Who made his shroud?"
"I," said the Beetle,
"With my thread and needle,
I made his shroud."—

—Death of Cock Robin

It must be much easier to play at things when there are more of you than when there is only one.

There is only one of me, and Nurse does not care about playing at things. Sometimes I try to persuade her; but if she is in a good temper she says she has got a bone in her leg, and if she isn't she says that when little boys can't amuse themselves it's a sure and certain sign they've got "the worrits," and the sooner they are put to bed with a Gregory's powder "the better for themselves and every one else."

Godfather Gilpin can play delightfully when he has time, and he believes in fancy things, only he is so very busy with his books. But even when he is reading he will let you put him in the game. He doesn't mind pretending to be a fancy person if he hasn't to do anything, and if I do speak to him he always remembers who he is. That is why I like playing in his study better than in the nursery. And Nurse always says "He's safe enough, with the old gentleman," so I'm allowed to go there as much as I like.

Godfather Gilpin lets me play with the books, because I always take care of them. Besides, there is nothing else to play with, except the window-curtains, for the chairs are always full. So I sit on the floor, and sometimes I build with the books (particularly Stonehenge), and sometimes I make people of them, and call them by the names on their backs, and the ones in other languages we call foreigners, and Godfather Gilpin tells me what countries they belong to. And sometimes I lie on my face and read (for I could read when I was four years old), and Godfather Gilpin tells me the hard words. The only rule he makes is, that I must get all the books out of one shelf, so that they are easily put away again. I may have any shelf I like, but I must not mix the shelves up.

I always took care of the books, and never had any accident with any of them till the day I dropped Jeremy Taylor's *Sermons*. It made me very miserable, because I knew that Godfather Gilpin could never trust me so much again.

However, if it had not happened, I should not have known anything about the Brothers of Pity; so, perhaps (as Mrs. James, Godfather Gilpin's house-keeper, says), "All's for the best," and "It's an ill wind that blows nobody good."

It happened on a Sunday, I remember, and it was the day after the day on which I had had the shelf in which all the books were alike. They were all foreigners—Italians—and

Juliana Horatia Ewing

all their names were *Goldoni*, and there were forty-seven of them, and they were all in white and gold. I could not read any of them, but there were lots of pictures, only I did not know what the stories were about. So next day, when Godfather Gilpin gave me leave to play a Sunday game with the books, I thought I would have English ones, and big ones, for a change, for the *Goldonis* were rather small.

We played at church, and I was the parson, and Godfather Gilpin was the old gentleman who sits in the big pew with the knocker, and goes to sleep (because he wanted to go to sleep), and the books were the congregation. They were all big, but some of them were fat, and some of them were thin, like real people—not like the *Goldonis*, which were all alike.

I was arranging them in their places and looking at their names, when I saw that one of them was called Taylor's *Sermons*, and I thought I would keep that one out and preach a real sermon out of it when I had read prayers. Of course I had to do the responses as well as "Dearly beloved brethren" and those things, and I had to sing the hymns too, for the books could not do anything, and Godfather Gilpin was asleep.

When I had finished the service I stood behind a chair that was full of newspapers, for a pulpit, and I lifted up Taylor's *Sermons*, and rested it against the chair, and began to look to see what I would preach. It was an old book, bound in brown leather, and ornamented with gold, with a picture of a man in a black gown and a round black cap and a white collar in the beginning; and there was a list of all the sermons with their names and the texts. I read it through, to see which sounded the most interesting, and I didn't care much for any of them. However, the last but one was called "A Funeral Sermon, preached at the Obsequies of the Right Honourable the Countess of Carbery;" and I wondered what obsequies were, and who the Countess of Carbery was, and I thought I would preach that sermon and try to find out.

There was a very long text, and it was not a very easy one. It was: "For we must needs die, and are as water spilt on the ground, which cannot be gathered up again: neither doth GOD respect any person: yet doth He devise means that His banished be not expelled from Him."

The sermon wasn't any easier than the text, and half the *s*'s were like *f*'s which made it rather hard to preach, and there was Latin mixed up with it, which I had to skip. I had preached two pages when I got into the middle of a long sentence, of which part was this: "Every trifling accident discomposes us; and as the face of waters wafting in a storm so wrinkles itself, that it makes upon its forehead furrows deep and hollow like a grave: so do our great and little cares and trifles first make the wrinkles of old age, and then they dig a grave for us."

I knew the meaning of the words "wrinkles," and "old age." Godfather Gilpin's forehead had unusually deep furrows, and, almost against my will, I turned so quickly to look if his wrinkles were at all like the graves in the churchyard, that Taylor's *Sermons*, in its heavy binding, slipped from the pulpit and fell to the ground.

And Godfather Gilpin woke up, and (quite forgetting that he was really the old gentleman in the pew with the knocker) said, "Dear me, dear me! is that Jeremy Taylor that you are knocking about like a football? My dear child, I can't lend you my books to play with if you drop them on to the floor."

I took it up in my arms and carried it sorrowfully to Godfather Gilpin. He was very kind, and said it was not hurt, and I might go on playing with the others; but I could see

Juliana Horatia Ewing

him stroking its brown leather and gold back, as if it had been bruised and wanted comforting, and I was far too sorry about it to go on preaching, even if I had had anything to preach.

I picked up the smallest book I could see in the congregation, and sat down and pretended to read. There were pictures in it, but I turned over a great many, one after the other, before I could see any of them, my eyes were so full of tears of mortification and regret. The first picture I saw when my tears had dried up enough to let me see was a very curious one indeed. It was a picture of two men carrying what looked like another man covered with a blue quilt, on a sort of bier. But the funny part about it was the dress of the men. They were wrapped up in black cloaks, and had masks over their faces, and underneath the picture was written, "*Fratelli della Misericordia*"—"Brothers of Pity."

I do not know whether the accident to Jeremy Taylor had made Godfather Gilpin too anxious about his books to sleep, but I found that he was keeping awake, and after a bit he said to me, "What are you staring so hard and so quietly at, little Mouse?"

I looked at the back of the book, and it was called *Religious Orders*; so I said, "It's called *Religious Orders*, but the picture I'm looking at has got two men dressed in black, with their faces covered all but their eyes, and they are carrying another man with something blue over him."

"*Fratelli della Misericordia*," said Godfather Gilpin.

"Who are they, and what are they doing?" I asked. "And why are their faces covered?"

"They belong to a body of men," was Godfather Gilpin's

reply, "who bind themselves to be ready in their turn to do certain offices of mercy, pity, and compassion to the sick, the dying, and the dead. The brotherhood is six hundred years old, and still exists. The men who belong to it receive no pay, and they equally reject the reward of public praise, for they work with covered faces, and are not known even to each other. Rich men and poor men, noble men and working men, men of letters and the ignorant, all belong to it, and each takes his turn when it comes round to nurse the sick, carry the dying to hospital, and bury the dead.'

"Is that a dead man under the blue coverlet?" I asked with awe.

"I suppose so," said Godfather Gilpin.

"But why don't his friends go to the funeral?" I inquired.

"He has no friends to follow him," said my godfather. "That is why he is being buried by the Brothers of Pity."

Long after Godfather Gilpin had told me all that he could tell me of the *Fratelli della Misericordia*—long after I had put the congregation (including the *Religious Orders* and Taylor's *Sermons*) back into the shelf to which they belonged —the masked faces and solemn garb of the men in the picture haunted me.

I have changed my mind a great many times, since I can remember, about what I will be when I am grown up. Sometimes I have thought I should like to be an officer and die in battle; sometimes I settled to be a clergyman and preach splendid sermons to enormous congregations; once I quite decided to be a head fireman and wear a brass helmet, and be whirled down lighted streets at night, every one making way for me, on errands of life and death.

Juliana Horatia Ewing

But the history of the Brothers of Pity put me out of conceit with all other heroes. It seemed better than anything I had ever thought of—to do good works unseen of men, without hope of reward, and to those who could make no return. For it rang in my ears that Godfather Gilpin had said, "He has no friends—that is why he is being buried by the Brothers of Pity."

I quite understood what I thought they must feel, because I had once buried a cat who had no friends. It was a poor half-starved old thing, for the people it belonged to had left it, and I used to see it slinking up to the back door and looking at Tabby, who was very fat and sleek, and at the scraps on the unwashed dishes after dinner. Mrs. Jones kicked it out every time, and what happened to it before I found it lying draggled and dead at the bottom of the Ha-ha, with the top of a kettle still fastened to its scraggy tail, I never knew, and it cost me bitter tears to guess. It cost me some hard work, too, to dig the grave, for my spade was so very small.

I don't think Mrs. Jones would have cared to be a Brother of Pity, for she was very angry with me for burying that cat, because it was such a wretched one, and so thin and dirty, and looked so ugly and smelt so nasty. But that was just why I wanted to give it a good funeral, and why I picked my crimson lily and put it in the grave, because it seemed so sad the poor thing should be like that when it might have been clean and fluffy, and fat and comfortable, like Tabby, if it had had a home and people to look after it.

It was remembering about the cat that made me think that there were no Brothers of Pity (not even in Tuscany, for I asked Godfather Gilpin) to bury beasts and birds and fishes when they have no friends to go to their funerals. And that was how it was that I settled to be a Brother of Pity without waiting till I grew up and could carry men.

I had a shilling of my own, and with sixpence of it I bought a yard and a half of black calico at the post-office shop, and Mrs. Jones made me a cloak out of it; and with the other sixpence I bought a mask—for they sell toys there too. It was not a right sort of mask, but I could not make Mrs. Jones understand about a hood with two eye-holes in it, and I did not like to show her the picture, for if she had seen that I wanted to play at burying people, perhaps she would not have made me the cloak. She made it very well, and it came down to my ankles, and I could hide my spade under it. The worst of the mask was that it was a funny one, with a big nose; but it hid my face all the same, and when you get inside a mask you can feel quite grave whatever it's painted like.

I had never had so happy a summer before as the one when I was a Brother of Pity. I heard Nurse saying to Mrs. Jones that "there was no telling what would keep children out of mischief," for that I "never seemed to be tired of that old black rag and that ridiculous face."

But it was not the dressing-up that pleased me day after day, it was the chance of finding dead bodies with no friends to bury them. Going out is quite a new thing when you have something to look for; and Godfather Gilpin says he felt just the same in the days when he used to collect insects.

I found a good many corpses of one sort and another: birds and mice and frogs and beetles, and sometimes bigger bodies—such as kittens and dogs. The stand of my old wooden horse made a capital thing to drag them on, for all the wheels were there, and I had a piece of blue cotton-velvet to put on the top, but the day I found a dead mole I did not cover him. I put him outside, and he looked like black velvet lying on blue velvet. It seemed quite a pity to put him into the dirty ground, with such a lovely coat.

Juliana Horatia Ewing

One day I was coming back from burying a mouse, and I saw a "flying watchman" beetle lying quite stiff and dead, as I thought, with his legs stretched out, and no friends; so I put him on the bier at once, and put the blue velvet over him, and drew him to the place where the mouse's grave was. When I took the pall off and felt him, and turned him over and over, he was still quite rigid, so I felt sure he was dead, and began to dig his grave; but when I had finished and went back to the bier, the flying watchman was just creeping over the wheel. He had only pretended to be dead, and had given me all that trouble for nothing.

When first I became a Brother of Pity, I thought I would have a graveyard to bury all the creatures in, but afterwards I changed my mind and settled to bury them all near wherever I found them. But I got some bits of white wood, and fastened them across each other with bits of wire, and so marked every grave.

At last there were lots of them dotted about the fields and woods I knew. I remembered to whom most of them belonged, and even if I had forgotten, it made a very good game, to pretend to be a stranger in the neighbourhood, and then pretend to be somebody else, talking to myself, and saying, "Wherever you see those little graves some poor creature has been buried by the Brothers of Pity."

I did not like to read the burial service, for fear it should not be quite right (especially for frogs; there were so many of them in summer, and they were so horrid-looking, I used to bury several together, and pretend it was the time of the plague); but I did not like not having any service at all. So when I put on my cloak and mask, and took my spade and the bier, I said, "Brothers, let us prepare to perform this work of mercy," which is the first thing the real *Fratelli della Misericordia* say when they are going out. And when I buried the body I said, "Go in peace," which is the last thing that they say. Godfather Gilpin told me, and I learnt it by heart.

I enjoyed it very much. There were graves of beasts and birds who had died without friends in the hedges and the soft parts of the fields in almost all our walks. I never showed them to Nurse, but I often wondered that she did not notice them. I always touched my hat when I passed them, and sometimes it was very difficult to do so without her seeing me, but it made me quite uncomfortable if I passed a grave without. When I could not find any bodies I amused myself with making wreaths to hang over particularly nice poor beasts, such as a bullfinch or a kitten.

I had been a Brother of Pity for several months, when a very curious thing happened.

One summer evening I went by myself after tea into a steep little field at the back of our house, with an old stone-quarry at the top, on the ledges of which, where the earth had settled, I used to play at making gardens. And there, lying on a bit of very stony ground, half on the stones and half on the grass, was a dead robin-redbreast. I love robins very much, and it was not because I wanted one to die, but because I thought that if one did die, I should so like to bury him, that I had wished to find a dead robin ever since I became a Brother of Pity. It was rather late, but it wanted nearly an hour to my usual bedtime, so I thought I would go home at once for my dress and spade and bier, and for some roses. For I had resolved to bury this (my first robin-redbreast) in a grave lined with rose-leaves, and to give him a wreath of forget-me-nots.

Just as I was going I heard a loud buzz above my head, and something hit me in the face. It was a beetle, whirring about

Juliana Horatia Ewing

in the air, and as I turned to leave poor Robin the beetle sat down on him, on the middle of his red breast, and by still hearing the buzzing, I found that another beetle was whirling and whirring just above my head in the air. I like beetles (especially the flying watchmen), and these ones were black too; so I said, for fun, "You've got on your black things, and if you'll take care of the body till I get my spade you shall be Brothers of Pity."

I ran home, and I need not have gone indoors at all, for I keep my cloak and my spade and the bier in the summer-house, but the bits of wood were in the nursery cupboard, so, after I had got some good roses, and was quite ready, I ran up-stairs, and there, to my great vexation, Nurse met me, and said I was to go to bed.

I thought it was very hard, because it had been a very hot day, and I had had to go a walk in the heat of the sun along the old coaching-road with Nurse, and it seemed so provoking, now it was cool and the moon was rising, that I should have to go to bed, especially as Nurse was sending me there earlier than usual because she wanted to go out herself, and I knew it.

I tried to go to sleep, but I couldn't. Every time I opened my eyes the moonlight was more and more like daylight through the white blind. At last I almost thought I must have really been to sleep without knowing it, and that it must be morning. So I got out of bed, and went to the window and peeped; but it was still moonlight—only moonlight as bright as day—and I saw Nurse and two of the maids just going through the upper gate into the park.

In one moment I made up my mind. Nurse had only put me to bed to get me out of the way. I did not mean to trouble her, but I was determined not to lose the chance of being

Brother of Pity to a robin-redbreast.

I dressed myself as well as I could, got out unobserved, and made my way to the summer-house. Things look a little paler by moonlight, otherwise I could see quite well. I put on my cloak, took my spade and the handle of the bier in my right hand, and holding the mask over my face with my left, I made my way to the quarry field.

It was a lovely night, and as I strolled along I thought with myself that the ground where Robin lay was too stony for my spade, and that I must move him a little lower, where some soft earth bordered one side of the quarry.

I was as certain as I had ever been of anything that I did not think about this till then, but when I got to the quarry the body was gone from the place where I had found it; and when I looked lower, on the bit of soft earth there lay Robin, just in the place where I was settling in my mind that I would bury him.

I could not believe my eyes through the holes in my mask, so I pulled it off, but there was no doubt about the fact. There he lay; and round him, when I looked closer, I saw a ridge like a rampart of earth, which framed him neatly and evenly, as if he were already halfway into his grave.

The moonlight was as clear as day, there was no mistake as to what I saw, and whilst I was looking the body of the bird began to sink by little jerks, as if some one were pulling it from below. When first it moved I thought that poor Robin could not be dead after all, and that he was coming to life again like the flying watchman, but I soon saw that he was not, and that some one was pulling him down into a grave.

When I felt quite sure of this, when I had rubbed my eyes to

Juliana Horatia Ewing

clear them, and pulled up the lashes to see if I was awake, I was so horribly frightened that, with my mask in one hand and the spade and the handle of my bier in the other, I ran home as fast as my legs would carry me, leaving the roses and the cross and the blue-velvet pall behind me in the quarry.

Nurse was still out; and I crept back to bed without detection, where I dreamed disturbedly of invisible grave-diggers all through the night.

I did not feel quite so much afraid by daylight, but I was not a bit less puzzled as to how Cock Robin had been moved from the stony place to the soft earth, and who dug his grave. I could not ask Nurse about it, for I should have had to tell her I had been out, and I could not have trusted Mrs. Jones either; but Godfather Gilpin never tells tales of me, and he knows everything, so I went to him.

The more I thought of it the more I saw that the only way was to tell him everything; for if you only tell parts of things you sometimes find yourself telling lies before you know where you are. So I put on my cloak and my mask, and took the shovel and bier into the study, and sat down on the little foot-stool I always wait on when Godfather Gilpin is in the middle of reading, and keeps his head down to show that he does not want to be disturbed.

When he shut up his book and looked at me he burst out laughing. I meant to have asked him why, but I was so busy afterwards I forgot. I suppose it was the nose, for it had got rather broken when I fell down as I was burying the old drake that Neptune killed.

But he was very kind to me, and I told him all about my being a Brother of Pity, and how I had wanted to bury a robin, and how I had found one, and how he had frightened me by burying himself.

"Some other Brother of Pity must have found him," said my godfather, still laughing. "And he must have got Jack the Giant-killer's cloak of darkness for *his* dress, so that you did not see him."

"There was nobody there," I earnestly answered, shaking my mask as I thought of the still, lonely moonlight. "Nothing but two beetles, and I said if they would take care of him they might be Brothers of Pity."

"They took you at your word, *mio fratello*. Take off your mask, which a little distracts me, and I will tell you who buried Cock Robin."

I knew when Godfather Gilpin was really telling me things— without thinking of something else, I mean,—and I listened with all my ears.

"The beetles whom you very properly admitted into your brotherhood," said my godfather, "were burying beetles, or sexton beetles,[A] as they are sometimes called. They bury animals of all sizes in a surprisingly short space of time. If two of them cannot conduct the funeral, they summon others. They carry the bodies, if necessary, to suitable ground. With their flat heads (for the sexton beetle does not carry a shovel as you do) they dig trench below trench all round the body they are committing to the earth, after which they creep under it and pull it down, and then shovel away once more, and so on till it is deep enough in, and then they push the earth over it and tread it and pat it neatly down."

"Then was it the beetles who were burying the robin-redbreast?" I gasped.

"I suspect so," said Godfather Gilpin. "But we will go and see."

He actually knocked a book down in his hurry to get his hat, and when I helped him to pick it up, and said, "Why, godfather, you're as bad as I was about Taylor's *Sermons*," he said, "I am an old fool, my dear. I used to be very fond of insects before I settled down to the work I'm at now, and it quite excites me to go out into the fields again."

I never had a nicer walk, for he showed me lots of things I had never noticed, before we got to the quarry field; and then I took him straight to the place where the bit of soft earth was, and there was nothing to be seen, and the earth was quite smooth and tidy. But when he poked with his stick the ground was very soft, and after he had poked a little we saw some nut-brown feathers, and we knew it was Robin's grave.

And I said, "Don't poke any more, please. I wanted to bury him with rose-leaves, but the beetles were dressed in black, and I gave them leave, and I think I'll put a cross over him, because I don't think it's untrue to show that he was buried by the Brothers of Pity."

Godfather Gilpin quite agreed with me, and we made a nice mound (for I had brought my spade), and put the best kind of cross, and afterwards I made a wreath of forget-me-nots to hang on it.

He was the only robin-redbreast I have found since I became a Brother of Pity, and that was how it was that it was not I who buried him after all.

Many of the walks that Nurse likes to take I do not care about, but one place she likes to go to, especially on Sunday, I like too, and that is the churchyard.

I was always fond of it. It is so very nice to read the tombstones, and fancy what the people were like, particularly the ones who lived long ago, in 1600 and something, with beautifully-shaped sixes and capital letters on their graves. For they must have dressed quite differently from us, and perhaps they knew Charles the First and Oliver Cromwell.

Diggory the gravedigger never talks much, but I like to watch him. I think he is rather deaf, for when I asked him if he thought, if he went on long enough, he could dig himself through to the other side of the world, he only said "Hey?" and chucked up a great shovelful of earth. But perhaps it was because he was so deep down that he could not hear.

Now, when he is quite out of sight, and chucks the earth up like that, it makes me think of the sexton beetles; for Godfather Gilpin says they drive their flat heads straight down, and then lift them with a sharp jerk, and throw the earth up so.

I said to Diggory one day, "Don't you wish your head was flat, instead of being as it is, so that you could shovel with it instead of having to have a spade?"

He wasn't so deep down that time, and he heard me, and put his head up out of the grave and rested on his spade. But he only scratched his head and stared, and said, "You be an uncommon queer young gentleman, to be sure," and then went on digging again. And I was afraid he was angry, so I daren't ask him any more.

I daren't of course ask him if he is a Brother of Pity, but I think he deserves to be, for workhouse burials at any rate; for if you have only the Porter and Silly Billy at your funeral, I don't think you can call that having friends.

Juliana Horatia Ewing

I have taken the beetles for my brothers, of course. God-father Gilpin says I should find far more bodies than I do if they were not burying all along. I often wish I could understand them when they hum, and that they knew me.

I wonder if either they or Diggory know that they belong to the order of *Fratelli della Misericordia*, and that I belong to it too?

But of course it would not be right to ask them, even if either of them would answer me, for if we were "known, even to each other," we should not really and truly be Brothers of Pity.

> NOTE—Burying beetles are to the full as skilful as they are described in this tale. With a due respect for the graces of art, I have not embodied the fact that they feed on the carcases which they bury. The last thing that the burying beetle does, after tidying the grave, is to make a small hole and go down himself, having previously buried his partner with their prey. Here the eggs are laid, and the larvae hatched and fed.

FOOTNOTES:

[Footnote A: *Necrophorus humator*, &c.]

FATHER HEDGEHOG AND HIS NEIGHBOURS

* * * * *

CHAPTER I

The care of a large family is no light matter, as everybody knows. And that year I had an unusually large family. No less than seven young urchins for Mrs. Hedgehog and myself to take care of and start in life; and there was not a prickly parent on this side of the brook, or within three fields beyond, who had more than four.

My father's brother had six one year, I know. It was the summer that I myself was born. I can remember hearing my father and mother talk about it before I could see. As these six cousins were discussed in a tone of interest and respect which seemed to bear somewhat disparagingly on me and my brother and sisters (there were only four of *us*), I was rather glad to learn that they also had been born blind. My father used to go and see them, and report their progress to my mother on his return.

"They can see to-day."

"They have curled themselves up. Every one of them. Six

Juliana Horatia Ewing

beautiful little balls; as round as crab-apples and as safe as burrs!"

I tried to curl myself up, but I could only get my coat a little way over my nose. I cried with vexation. But one should not lose heart too easily. With patience and perseverance most things can be brought about, and I could soon both see and curl myself into a ball. It was about this time that my father hurried home one day, tossing the leaves at least three inches over his head as he bustled along.

"What in the hedge do you think has happened to the six?" said he.

"Oh, don't tell me!" cried my mother; "I am so nervous." (Which she was, and rather foolish as well, which used to irritate my father, who was hasty tempered, as I am myself.)

"They've been taken by gipsies and flitted," said he.

"What do you mean by *flitted*?" inquired my mother.

"A string is tied round a hind-leg of each, and they are tethered in the grass behind the tent, just as the donkey is tethered. So they will remain till they grow fat, and then they will be cooked."

"Will the donkey be cooked when he is fat?" asked my mother.

"I smell valerian," said my father; on which she put out her nose, and he ran at it with his prickles. He always did this when he was annoyed with any member of his family; and though we knew what was coming, we are all so fond of valerian, we could never resist the temptation to sniff, just on the chance of there being some about.

I had long wanted to see my cousins, and I now begged my father to let me go with him the next time he went to visit them. But he was rather cross that morning, and he ran at me with his back up.

"So you want to gad about and be kidnapped and flitted too, do you? Just let me—"

But when I saw him coming, I rolled myself up as tight as a wood-louse, and as my ears were inside I really did not hear what else he said. But I was not a whit the less resolved to see my cousins.

One day my father bustled home.

"Upon my whine," said he, "they live on the fat of the land. Scraps of all kinds, apples, and a dish of bread and milk under their very noses. I sat inside a gorse bush on the bank, and watched them till my mouth watered."

The next day he reported—

"They've cooked one—in clay. There are only five now."

And the next day—

"They've cooked another. Now there are only four."

"There won't be a cousin left if I wait much longer," thought I.

On the morrow there were only three.

My mother began to cry. "My poor dear nephews and nieces!" said she (though she had never seen them). "What a world this is!"

Juliana Horatia Ewing

"We must take it as we eat eggs," said my father, with that air of wisdom which naturally belongs to the sayings of the head of the family, "the shell with the yolk. And they have certainly had excellent victuals."

Next morning he went off as usual, and I crept stealthily after him. With his spines laid flat to his sides, and his legs well under him, he ran at a good round pace, and as he did not look back I followed him with impunity. By and by he climbed a bank and then crept into a furze bush, whose prickles were no match for his own. I dared not go right into the bush for fear he should see me, but I settled myself as well as I could under shelter of a furze branch, and looked down on to the other side of the bank, where my father's nose was also directed. And there I saw my three cousins, tethered as he had said, and apparently very busy over-eating themselves on food which they had not had the trouble of procuring.

If I had heard less about the cooking, I might have envied them; as it was, that somewhat voracious appetite charac-teristic of my family disturbed my judgment sufficiently to make me almost long to be flitted myself. I fancy it must have been when I pushed out my nose and sniffed involuntarily towards the victuals, that the gipsy man heard me.

He had been lying on the grass, looking much lazier than my cousins—which is saying a good deal—and only turning his swarthy face when the gipsy girl, as she moved about and tended the fire, got out of the sight of his eyes. Then he moved so that he could see her again; not, as it seemed, to see what she was doing or to help her to do it, but as leaves move with the wind, or as we unpacked our noses against our wills when my father said he smelt valerian.

She was very beautiful. Her skin was like a trout pool—clear and yet brown. I never saw any eyes like her eyes, though our neighbour's—the Water Rat—at times recalls them. Her hair was the colour of ripe blackberries in a hot hedge—very ripe ones, with the bloom on. She moved like a snake. I have seen my father chase a snake more than once, and I have seen a good many men and women in my time. Some of them walk like my father, they bustle along and kick up the leaves as he does; and some of them move quickly and yet softly, as snakes go. The gipsy girl moved so, and wherever she went the gipsy man's eyes went after her.

Suddenly he turned them on me. For an instant I was paralyzed and stood still. I could hear my father bustling down the bank; in a few minutes he would be at home, where my brother and sisters were safe and sound, whilst I was alone and about to reap the reward of my disobedience, in the fate of which he had warned me—to be taken by gipsies and flitted.

Nothing, my dear children—my seven dear children—is more fatal in an emergency than indecision. I was half disposed to hurry after my father, and half resolved to curl myself into a ball. I had one foot out and half my back rounded, when the gipsy man pinned me to the ground with a stick, and the gipsy girl strode up. I could not writhe myself away from the stick, but I gazed beseechingly at the gipsy girl and squealed for my life.

"Let the poor little brute go, Basil," she said, laughing. "We've three flitted still."

"Let it go?" cried the young man scornfully, and with another poke, which I thought had crushed me to bits, though I was still able to cry aloud.

Juliana Horatia Ewing

The gipsy girl turned her back and went away with one movement and without speaking.

"Sybil!" cried the man; but she did not look round.

"Sybil, I say!"

She was breaking sticks for the fire slowly across her knee, but she made no answer. He took his stick out of my back, and went after her.

"I've let it go," he said, throwing himself down again, "and a good dinner has gone with it. But you can do what you like with me—and small thanks I get for it."

"I can do anything with you but keep you out of mischief," she answered, fixing her eyes steadily on him. He sat up and began to throw stones, aiming them at my three cousins.

"Take me for good and all, instead of tormenting me, and you will," he said.

"Will you give up Jemmy and his gang?" she asked; but as he hesitated for an instant, she tossed the curls back from her face and moved away, saying, "Not you; for all your talk! And yet for your sake, *I* would give up—"

He bounded to his feet, but she had put the bonfire between them, and before he could get round it, she was on the other side of a tilted cart, where another woman, in a crimson cloak, sat doing something to a dirty pack of cards.

I did not like to see the gipsy man on his feet again, and having somewhat recovered breath, I scrambled down the bank and got home as quickly as the stiffness and soreness of my skin would allow.

I never saw my cousins again, and it was long before I saw any more gipsies; for that day's adventure gave me a shock to which my children owe the exceeding care and prudence that I display in the choice of our summer homes and winter retreats, and in repressing every tendency to a wandering disposition among the members of my family.

Juliana Horatia Ewing

CHAPTER II

That summer—I mean the summer when I had seven—we had the most charming home imaginable. It was in a wood, and on that side of the wood which is farthest from houses and highroads. Here it was bounded by a brook, and beyond this lay a fine pasture field.

There are fields and fields. I never wish to know a better field than this one. I seldom go out much till the evening, but if business should take one along the hedge in the heat of the sun, there are as juicy and refreshing crabs to be picked up under a tree about half-way down the south side, as the thirstiest creature could desire.

And when the glare and drought of midday have given place to the mild twilight of evening, and the grass is refreshingly damped with dew, and scents are strong, and the earth yields kindly to the nose, what beetles and lob-worms reward one's routing!

I am convinced that the fattest and stupidest slugs that live, live near the brook. I never knew one who found out I was eating him, till he was half-way down my throat. And just opposite to the place where I furnished your dear mother's nest, is a small plantation of burdocks, on the underside of which stick the best flavoured snails I am acquainted with, in such inexhaustible quantities, that a hedgehog might have fourteen children in a season, and not fear their coming short of provisions.

And in the early summer, in the long grass on the edge of the wood—but no! I will not speak of it.

My dear children, my seven dear children, may you never

know what it is to taste a pheasant's egg—to taste several pheasant's eggs, and to eat them, shells and all.

There are certain pleasures of which a parent may himself have partaken, but which, if he cannot reconcile them with his ideas of safety and propriety, he will do well not to allow his children even to hear of. I do not say that I wish I had never tasted a pheasant's egg myself, but, when I think of traps baited with valerian, of my great-uncle's great-coat nailed to the keeper's door, of the keeper's heavy-heeled boots, and of the impropriety of poaching, I feel, as a father, that it is desirable that you should never know that there are such things as eggs, and then you will be quite happy without them.

But it was not the abundant and varied supply of food which had determined my choice of our home: it was not even because no woodland bower could be more beautiful,—because the coppice foliage was fresh and tender overhead, and the old leaves soft and elastic to the prickles below,—because the young oaks sheltered us behind, and we had a charming outlook over the brook in front, between a gnarled alder and a young sycamore, whose embracing branches were the lintel of our doorway.

No. I chose this particular spot in this particular wood, because I had reason to believe it to be a somewhat neglected bit of what men call "property,"—because the bramble bushes were unbroken, the fallen leaves untrodden, the hyacinths and ragged-robins ungathered by human feet and hands,—because the old fern-fronds faded below the fresh green plumes,—because the violets ripened seed,—because the trees were unmarked by woodmen and overpopulated with birds, and the water-rat sat up in the sun with crossed paws and without a thought of danger,—because, in short, no birds'-nesting, fern-digging, flower-picking, leaf-mould-wanting, vermin-hunting creatures ever came hither to replenish their ferneries, gardens, cages, markets, and museums.

My feelings can therefore be imagined when I was roused from an afternoon nap one warm summer's day by the voices of men and women. Several possibilities came into my mind, and I imparted them to my wife.

"They may be keepers."

"They may be poachers."

"They may be boys birds'-nesting."

"They may be street-sellers of ferns, moss, and so forth."

"They may be collectors of specimens."

"They may be pic-nic-ers—people who bring salt twisted up in a bit of paper with them, and leave it behind when they go away. Don't let the children touch it!"

"They may be—and this is the worst that could happen—men collecting frogs, toads, newts, snails, *and hedgehogs* for the London markets. We must keep very quiet. They will go away at sunset."

I was quite wrong, and when I heard the slow wheels of a cart I knew it. They were none of these things, and they did not go away. They were travelling tinkers, and they settled down and made themselves at home within fifty yards of mine.

My nerves have never been strong since that day under the furze bush. My first impulse was to roll myself up so tightly that I got the cramp, whilst every spine on my back stood stiff with fright. But after a time I recovered myself, and took counsel with Mrs. Hedgehog.

"Two things," said she, "are most important. We must keep the children from gadding, and we must make them hold their tongues."

"They never can be so foolish as to wish to quit your side, my dear, in the circumstances," said I. But I was mistaken.

I know nothing more annoying to a father who has learned the danger of indiscreet curiosity in his youth, than to find his sons apparently quite uninfluenced by his valuable experience.

"What are tinkers like?" was the first thing said by each one of the seven on the subject.

"They are a set of people," I replied, in a voice as sour as a green crab, "who if they hear us talking, or catch us walking abroad, will kill your mother and me, and temper up two bits of clay and roll us up in them. Then they will put us into a fire to bake, and when the clay turns red they will take us out. The clay will fall off and our coats with it. What remains they will eat—as we eat snails. You seven will be flitted. That is, you will be pegged to the ground till you grow big." (I thought it well not to mention the bread and milk.) "Then they will kill and bake and eat you in the same fashion."

I think this frightened the children; but they would talk about the tinkers, though they dared not go near them.

"The best thing you can do," said Mrs. Hedgehog, "is to tell them a story to keep them quiet. You can modulate your own voice, and stop if you hear the tinkers."

Hereupon I told them a story (a very old one) of the hedgehog who ran a race with a hare, on opposite sides of a hedge, for the wager of a louis d'or and a bottle of brandy. It was a great favourite with them.

"The moral of the tale, my dear children," I was wont to say, "is, that our respected ancestor's head saved his heels, which is never the case with giddy-pated creatures like the hare."

"Perhaps it was a very young hare," said Mrs. Hedgehog, who is amiable, and does not like to blame any one if it can be avoided.

"I don't think it can have been a *very* young hare," said I, "or the hedgehog would have eaten him instead of outwitting him. As it was, he placed himself and Mrs. Hedgehog at opposite ends of the course. The hare started on one side of the hedge and the hedgehog on the other. Away went the hare like the wind, but Mr. Hedgehog took three steps and went back to his place. When the hare reached his end of the hedge, Mrs. Hedgehog, from the other side, called out, 'I'm here already.' Her voice and her coat were very like her husband's, and the hare was not observant enough to remark a slight difference of size and colour. The moral of which is, my dear children, that one must use his eyes as well as his legs in this world. The hare tried several runs, but there was always a hedgehog at the goal when he got there. So he gave in at last, and our ancestors walked comfortably home, taking the louis d'or and the bottle of brandy with them."

"What is a louis d'or?" cried three of my children; and "What is brandy?" asked the other four.

"I smell valerian," said I; on which they poked out their seven noses, and I ran at them with my spines, for a father who is not an Encyclopaedia on all fours must adopt *some* method of checking the inquisitiveness of the young.

When grown-up people desire information or take an interest in their neighbours, this, of course, is another matter. Mrs. Hedgehog and I had never seen tinkers, and we resolved to take an early opportunity some evening of sending the seven urchins down to the burdock plantations to pick snails, whilst we paid a cautious visit to the tinker camp.

But mothers are sad fidgets, and anxious as Mrs. Hedgehog was to gratify her curiosity, she kept putting off our expedition till the children's spines should be harder; so I made one or two careful ones by myself, and told her all the news on my return.

CHAPTER III

"The animal Man," so I have heard my uncle, who was a learned hedgehog, say,—"the animal man is a diurnal animal; he comes out and feeds in the daytime." But a second cousin, who had travelled as far as Covent Garden, and who lived for many years in a London kitchen, told me that he thought my uncle was wrong, and that man comes out and feeds at night. He said he knew of at least one house in which the crickets and black-beetles never got a quiet kitchen to themselves till it was nearly morning.

But I think my uncle was right about men in the country. I am sure the tinker and his family slept at night. He and his wife were out a great deal during the day. They went away from the wood and left the children with an old woman, who was the tinker's mother. At one time they were away for several days, and about my usual time for going out the children were asleep, and the old woman used to sit over the camp fire with her head on her hands.

"The language of men, my dear," I observed to Mrs. Hedgehog, "is quite different to ours, even in general tone; but I assure you that when I first heard the tinker's mother, I could have wagered a louis d'or and a bottle of brandy that I heard hedgehogs whining to each other. In fact, I was about to remonstrate with them for their imprudence, when I found out that it was the old woman who was moaning and muttering to herself."

"What is the matter with her?" asked Mrs. Hedgehog.

"I was curious to know myself," said I, "and from what I have overheard, I think I can inform you. She is the tinker's mother, and judging from what he said the other night, was not by any means indulgent to him when he was a child. She is harsh enough to his young brats now; but it appears that she was devoted to an older son, one of the children of his first wife; and that it is for the loss of this grandchild that she vexes herself."

"Is he dead?"

"No, my dear, but—"

"Has he been flitted?"

"Something of the kind, I fear. He has been taken to prison."

"Dear, dear!" said Mrs. Hedgehog; "what a trial to a mother's feelings! Will they bake him?"

"I think not," said I. "I fancy that he is tethered up as a punishment for taking what did not belong to him; and the grandmother's grievance seems to be that she believes he was unjustly convicted. She thinks the real robber was a gipsy. Just as if I were taken, and my skin nailed to the keeper's door for pheasant's eggs which I had never had the pleasure of eating."

Mrs. Hedgehog was now dying of curiosity. She said she thought the children's spines were strong enough for anything that was likely to happen to them; and so the next fresh damp evening we sent the seven urchins down to the burdocks to pick snails, and crept cautiously towards the tinker's encampment to see what we could see. And there, by the smouldering embers of a bonfire, sat the old woman moaning, as I had described her, with her elbows on her knees, rocking and nursing her head, from which her long hair was looped and fell, like grey rags, about her withered fingers.

"I don't like her looks," snorted Mrs. Hedgehog. "And how disgustingly they have trampled the grass."

"It is quite true," said I; "it will not recover itself this summer. I wish they had left us our wood to ourselves."

At this moment Mrs. Hedgehog laid her five toes on mine, to attract my attention, and whispered—"Is it a gipsy?" and lifting my nose in the direction of the rustling brushwood, I saw Sybil. There was no mistaking her, though her cheeks looked hollower and her eyes larger than when I saw her last.

"Good-evening, mother," she said.

The old woman raised her gaunt face with a start, and cried fiercely, "Begone with you! Begone!" and then bent it again upon her hands, muttering, "There are plenty of hedges and ditches too good for your lot, without their coming to worrit us in our wood."

The gipsy girl knelt quietly by the fire, and stirred up the embers.

"What is the matter, mother?" she said. "We've only just come, and when I heard that Tinker George and his mother were in the wood, I started to find you. 'You makes too free with the tinkers,' says my brother's wife. 'I goes to see my mother,' says I, 'who nursed me through a sickness, my real mother being dead, and my own people wanting to bury me through my not being able to speak or move, and their wanting to get to the Bartelmy Fair.' I never forget, mother; have you forgotten me, that you drives me away for bidding you good-day?"

"Good days are over for me," moaned the old woman. "Begone, I say! Don't let me see or hear any that belongs to

Black Basil, or it may be the worse for them."

("The tinker-mother whines very nastily," said Mrs. Hedgehog. "If I were the young woman, I should bite her."

"Hush!" I answered, "she is speaking.")

"Basil is in prison," said the gipsy girl hoarsely.

The old woman's eyes shone in their sockets, as she looked up at Sybil for a minute, as if to read the gipsy's sentence on her face; and then she chuckled,

"So they've taken the Terror of the Roads?"

Sybil's eyes had not moved from the fire, before which she was now standing with clasped hands.

"The Terror of the Roads?" she said. "Yes, they call him that,—but I could turn him round my finger, mother." Her voice had dropped, and she smoothed one of her black curls absently round her finger as she spoke.

"You couldn't keep him out of prison," taunted the old woman.

"I couldn't keep him out of mischief," said the girl, sadly; and then, with a sudden flash of anger, she clasped her hands above her head and cried, "A black curse on Jemmy and his gang!"

"A black curse on them as lets the innocent go to prison in their stead. They comes there themselves in the end, and long may it hold them!" was the reply.

Sybil moved swiftly to the old woman's side.

Juliana Horatia Ewing

"I heard you was in trouble, mother, about Christian; but you don't think—"

"*Think!*" screamed the old woman, shaking her fists, whilst the girl interrupted her—

"Hush, mother, hush! tell me now, tell me all, but not so loud," and kneeling with her back to us, she said something more in a low voice, to which the old woman replied in a whine so much moderated, that though Mrs. Hedgehog and I strained our ears, and crept as near the group as we dared, we could not catch a word.

Only, after a while Sybil rose up and walked back slowly to the fire, twisting the long lock of her hair as before, and saying—"I turns him round my finger, mother, as far as *that* goes—"

"So you thinks," said the old crone. "But he never will— even if you would, Sybil Stanley! Oh Christian, my child, my child!"

The gipsy girl stood still, like a young poplar-tree in the dead calm before thunder; and there fell a silence, in which I dared not have moved myself, or allowed Mrs. Hedgehog to move, three steps through the softest grass, for fear of being heard.

Then Sybil said abruptly, "I've never rightly heard about Christian, mother. What was it made you think so much more of him than you thinks about the others?"

CHAPTER IV

"My son's first wife died after Christian was born," said the old woman. "I've a sharp tongue, as you know, Sybil Stanley, and I'm doubtful if she was too happy while she lived; but when she was gone I knew she'd been a good 'un, and I've always spoken of her accordingly.

"You're too young to remember that year; it was a year of slack trade and hard times all over. Farmer-folk grudged you fourpence to mend the kettle, and as to broken victuals, there wasn't as much went in at the front door to feed the family, as the servants would have thrown out at the back door another year to feed the pigs.

"When one gets old, my daughter, and sits over the fire at night and thinks, instead of tramping all day and sleeping heavy after it, as one does when one is young—things comes back; things comes back, I say, as they says ghosts does.

"And when we camps near trees with long branches, like them over there, that waves in the wind and confuses your eyes among the smoke, I sometimes think I sees her face, as it was before she died, with a pinched look across the nose. That is Christian's mother, my son's first wife; and it comes back to me that I believes she starved herself to let him have more; for he's a man with a surly temper, like my own, is my son George. He grumbled worse than the children when he was hungry, and because she was so slow in getting strong enough to stand on her legs and carry the basket. You see he didn't hold his tongue when things were bad to bear, as she could. Men doesn't, my daughter."

"I know, I know," said the girl.

Juliana Horatia Ewing

"I thinks I was jealous of her," muttered the old woman; "it comes back to me that I begrudged her making so much of my son, but I knows now that she was a good 'un, and I speaks of her accordingly. She fretted herself about getting strong enough to carry the child to be christened, while we had the convenience of a parson near at hand, and I wasn't going to oblige her; but the day after she died, the child was ailing, and thinking it might require the benefit of a burial-service as well as herself, I wrapped it up, and made myself decent, and took my way to the village. I was half-way up the street, when I met a young gentlewoman in a grey dress coming out of a cottage.

"'Good-day, my pretty lady,' says I. 'Could you show an old woman the residence of the clergyman that would do the poor tinkers the kindness of christening a sick child whose mother lies dead in a tilted cart at the meeting of the four roads?'

"'I'm the clergyman's wife,' says she, with the colour in her face, 'and I'm sure my husband will christen the poor baby. Do let me see it.'"

"'It's only a tinker's child,' says I, 'a poor brown-faced morsel for a pretty lady's blue eyes to rest upon, that's accustomed to the delicate sight of her own golden-haired children; long may they live, and many may you and the gentle clergyman have of them!'"

"'I have no children,' says she, shortly, with the colour in her face breaking up into red and white patches over her cheeks. 'Let me carry the baby for you,' says she, a taking it from me. 'You must be tired.'"

"All the way she kept looking at it, and saying how pretty it was, and what beautiful long eyelashes it had, which went against me at the time, my daughter, for I knowed it was like its mother."

"The clergyman was a pleasing young gentleman of a genteel appearance, with a great deal to say for himself in the way of religion, as was right, it being his business. 'Name this child,' says he, and she gives a start that nobody sees but myself. So, thinking that the child being likely to die, there was no loss in obliging the gentlefolk, says I, looking down into the book as if I could read, 'Any name the lady thinks suitable for the poor tinker's child;' and says she, the colour coming up into her face, 'Call him Christian, for he shall be one.' So he was named Christian, a name to give no manner of displeasure to myself or to my family; it having been that of my husband's father, who was unfortunate in a matter of horse-stealing, and died across the water."

"What did *she* want with naming the baby, mother?" asked Sybil.

"I comes to that, my daughter, I comes to that, though it's hard to speak of. I hate myself worse than I hates the police when I thinks of it. But ten pounds—pieces of gold, my daughter, when half-pence were hard to come by—and small expectation that he would outlive his mother by many days—and a feeling against him then, for her sake, though I thinks differently now—"

"You sold him to the clergy-folks?" said Sybil.

"Ten pieces of gold! You never felt the pains of starvation, my daughter—nor perhaps those of jealousy, which are worse. The young clergywoman had no children, on which score she fretted herself; and must have fretted hard, before she begged the poor tinker's child out of the woods."

Juliana Horatia Ewing

"What did Tinker George say?" asked the girl.

"He used a good deal of bad language, and said I might as easily have got twenty pounds as ten, if I had not been as big a fool as the child's mother herself. Men are strange creatures, my daughter."

"So you left Christian with them?"

"I did, my daughter. I left him in the arms of the young clergywoman with the politest of words on both sides, and a good deal of religious conversation from the parson, which I does not doubt was well meant, if it was somewhat tedious."

"And then—mother?"

"And then we moved to Banbury, where my son took his second wife, having made her acquaintance in an alehouse; and then, my daughter, I begins to know that Christian's mother had been a good 'un."

"George isn't as happy with this one, then?"

"Men are curious creatures, my daughter, as you will discover for your own part without any instructions from me. He treats her far better than the other, because she treats him so much worse. But between them they soon put me a-one-side, and when I sat long evenings alone, sometimes in a wood, as it might be this, where the branches waves and makes a confusion of the shadows—and sometimes on the edge of a Hampshire heath where we camps a good deal, and the light is as slow in dying out of the bottom of the sky as he and she are in coming home, and the bits of water looks as if people had drownded themselves in them—when I sat alone, I say, minding the fire and the children—I wondered if Christian had lived, till I was all but mad with wondering and coming no nearer to knowing.

"'His mother was a good daughter to you,' I thinks; 'and if you hadn't sold him—sold your own flesh and blood—for ten golden sovereigns to the clergywoman, he might have been a good son to your old age.'"

"At last I could bear idleness and the lone company of my own thoughts no longer, my daughter, and I sets off to travel on my own account, taking money at back-doors, and living on broken meats I begged into the bargain, and working at nights instead of thinking. I knows a few arts, my daughter, of one sort and another, and I puts away most of what I takes, and changes it when the copper comes to silver, and *the silver comes to gold.*"

"I wonder you never went to see if he was alive," said Sybil.

"I did, my daughter. I went several times under various disguisements, which are no difficulty to those who know how to adopt them, and with servant's jewellery and children's toys, I had sight of him more than once, and each time made me wilder to get him back."

"And you never tried?"

"The money was not ready. One must act honourably, my daughter. I couldn't pick up my own grandson as if he'd been a stray hen, or a few clothes off the line. It took me five years to save those ten pounds. Five long miserable years."

"Miserable!" cried the gipsy girl, flinging her hair back from her eyes. "Miserable! Happy, you mean; too happy! It is when one can do nothing—"

She stopped, as if talking choked her, and the old woman,

Juliana Horatia Ewing

who seemed to pay little attention to any one but herself, went on,

"It was when it was all but saved, and I hangs about that country, making up my plans, that he comes to me himself, as I sits on the outskirts of a wood beyond the village, in no manner of disguisement, but just as I sits here."

"He came to you?" said Sybil.

"He comes to me, my daughter; dressed like any young nobleman of eight years old, but bareheaded and barefooted, having his cap in one hand, and his boots and stockings in the other."

"'Good-morning, old gipsy woman,' says he. 'I heard there was an old gipsy woman in the wood; so I came to see. Nurse said if I went about in the fields, by myself, the gipsies would steal me; but I told her I didn't care if they did, because it must be so nice to live in a wood, and sleep out of doors all night. When I grow up, I mean to be a wild man on a desert island, and dress in goats' skins. I sha'n't wear hats— I hate them; and I don't like shoes and stockings either. When I can get away from Nurse, I always take them off. I like to feel what I'm walking on, and in the wood I like to scuffle with my toes in the dead leaves. There's a quarry at the top of this wood, and I should so have liked to have thrown my shoes and stockings and my cap into it; but it vexes mother when I destroy my clothes, so I didn't, and I am carrying them.'"

"Those were the very words he said, my daughter. He had a swiftness of tongue, for which I am myself famous, especially in fortune-telling; but he used the language of gentility, and a shortness of speech which you will observe among those who are accustomed to order what they want instead of asking for it. I had hard work to summon voice to reply to him, my daughter, and I cannot tell you, nor would you understand it if I could find the words, what were my feelings to hear him speak with that confidence of the young clergywoman as his mother.

"'A green welcome to the woods and the fields, my noble little gentleman,' says I. 'Be pleased to honour the poor tinker-woman by accepting the refreshment of a seat and a cup of tea.'"

"'I mayn't eat or drink anything when I am visiting the poor people,' says he, 'Mother doesn't allow me. But thank you all the same, and please don't give me your stool, for I'd much rather sit on the grass; and, if you please, I should like you to tell me all about living in woods, and making fires, and hanging kettles on sticks, and going about the country and sleeping out of doors.'"

"Did you tell him the truth, or make up a tale for him?" asked Sybil.

"Partly one and partly the other, my daughter. But when persons sets their minds on anything, they sees the truth in a manner according to their own thoughts, which is of itself as good as a made-up tale."

"He asks numberless questions, to which I makes suitable replies. Them that lives out of doors—can they get up as early as they likes, without being called? he asks.

"Does gipsies go to bed in their clothes?

"Does they sometimes forget their prayers, with not regularly dressing and undressing?

"Did I ever sleep on heather?"

"Does we ever travel by moonlight?"

"Do I see the sun rise every morning?"

"Did I ever meet a highwayman?"

"Does I believe in ghosts?"

"Can I really tell fortunes?"

"I takes his shapely little hand—as brown as your own, my daughter, for his mother, like myself, was a pure Roman, and looked down upon by her people in consequence for marrying my son, who is of mixed blood (my husband being in family, as in every other respect, undeserving of the slightest mention)."

"'Let me tell you your fortune, my noble little gentleman,' I says. 'The lines of life are crossed early with those of travelling. Far will you wander, and many things will you see. Stone houses and houses of brick will not detain you. In the big house with the blue roof and the green carpet were you born, and in the big house with the blue roof and the green carpet will you die. The big house is delicately perfumed, my noble little gentleman, especially in the month of May; at which time there is also an abundance of music, and the singers sits overhead. Give the old gipsy woman a sight of your comely feet, my little gentleman, by the soles of which it is not difficult to see that you were born to wander.'"

"With this and similar jaw I entertained him, my daughter, and his eyes looks up at me out of his face till I feels as if the dead had come back; but he had a way with him besides which frightened me, for I knew that it came from living with gentlefolk."

"'Are you mighty learned, my dear?' says I. 'Are you well instructed in books and schooling?'"

"'I can say the English History in verse,' he says, 'and I do compound addition; and I know my Catechism, and lots of hymns. Would you like to hear me?'"

"'If you please, my little gentleman,' I says."

"'What shall I say?' he asks. 'I know all the English History, only I am not always quite sure how the kings come; but if you know the kings and can just give me the name, I know the verses quite well. And I know the Catechism perfectly, but perhaps you don't know the questions without the book. The hymns of course you don't want a book for, and I know them best of all.'"

"'I am not learned, myself,' says I, 'and I only know of two kings—the king of England—who, for that matter, is a queen, and a very good woman, they say, if one could come at her—and the king of the gipsies, who is as big a blackguard as you could desire to know, and by no means entitled to call himself king, though he gets a lot of money by it, which he spends in the public-house. As regards the other thing, my dear, I certainly does not know the questions without the book, nor, indeed, should I know them with the book, which is neither here nor there; so if the hymns require no learning on my part, I gives the preference to them.'"

"'I like *them* best, myself,' he says; and he puts his hat and his shoes and stockings on the ground, and stands up and folds his hands behind his back, and repeats a large number of religious verses, with the same readiness with which the young clergyman speaks out of a book."

"It partly went against me, my daughter, for I am not religious myself, and he was always too fond of holy words, which I thinks brings ill-luck. But his voice was as sweet as a thrush that sits singing in a thorn-bush, and between that and a something in the verses which had a tendency to make you feel uncomfortable, I feels more disturbed than I cares to show. But oh, my daughter, how I loves him!"

"'The blessing of an old gipsy woman on your young head,' I says. 'Fair be the skies under which you wanders, and shady the spots in which you rests!"

"'May the water be clear and the wood dry where you camps!"

"'May every road you treads have turf by the wayside, and the patteran[B] of a friend on the left.'"

"'What is the patteran?' he asks."

"'It is a secret,' I says, looking somewhat sternly at him. 'The roads keeps it, and the hedges keeps it—'"

"'I can keep it,' he says boldly. 'Pinch my finger, and try me!'"

"As he speaks he holds out his little finger, and I pinches it, my daughter, till the colour dies out of his lips, though he keeps them set, for I delights to see the nobleness and the endurance of him. So I explains the patteran to him, and shows him ours with two bits of hawthorn laid crosswise, for I does not regard him as a stranger, and I sees that he can keep his lips shut when it is required."

"He was practising the patteran at my feet, when I hears the cry of 'Christian!' and I cannot explain to you the chill that came over my heart at the sound.

"Trouble and age and the lone company of your own thoughts, my daughter, has a tendency to confuse you; and I am not by any means rightly certain at times about things I sees and hears. I sees Christian's mother when I knows she can't be there, and though I believes now that only one person was calling the child, yet, with the echo that comes from the quarry, and with worse than twenty echoes in my own mind, it seems to me that the wood is full of voices calling him."

"In my foolishness, my daughter, I sits like a stone, and he springs to his feet, and snatches up his things, and says, 'Good-bye, old gipsy woman, and thank you very much. I should like to stay with you,' he says, 'but Nurse is calling me, and Mother does get so frightened if I am long away and she doesn't know where. But I shall come back.'"

"I never quite knows, my daughter, whether it was the echo that repeated his words, or whether it was my own voice I hears, as I stretches my old arms after him, crying, 'Come back!'"

"But he runs off shouting, 'Coming, coming!'"

"And the wood deafens me, it is so full of voices."

"*Christian! Christian!—Coming! Coming!*"

"And I thinks I has some kind of a fit, my daughter, for when I wakes, the wood is as still as death, and he is gone, as dreams goes."

Juliana Horatia Ewing

CHAPTER V

"I really feel for the tinker-mother," whispered Mrs. Hedgehog.

"I feel for her myself," was my reply. "The cares of a family are heavy enough when they only last for the season, and one sleeps them off in a winter's nap. When—as in the case of men—they last for a lifetime, and you never get more than one night's rest at a time, they must be almost unendurable. As to prolonging one's anxieties from one's own families to the families of each of one's children—no parent in his senses—"

"What is the gipsy girl saying now?" asked Mrs. Hedgehog, who had been paying more attention to the women than to my observations—an annoyance to which, as head of the family, I have been subjected oftener than is becoming.

Sybil had been kneeling at the old woman's feet, soothing her and chafing her hands. At last she said,

"But you did get him, Mother. How was it?"

"Not for five more years, my daughter. And never in all that time could I get a sight of his face. The very first house I calls at next morning, I sees a chalk mark on the gate-post, placed there by some travelling tinker or pedler or what not, by which I knows that the neighbourhood is being made too hot for tramps and vagrants, as they call us. And go back in what disguisement I might, there was no selling a bootlace, nor begging a crust of bread there—*there*, where *he* lived.

"I makes up the ten pounds, and ties it in a bag; but I gets worse and worse in health and spirits and in confusion of mind, my daughter; and when I comes accidentally across my son in a Bedfordshire lane, and his wife is drinking, and he is in much bewilderment with the children, I takes up again with them, and I was with them when Christian comes to me the second time."

"He came back to you?"

"Learning and the confinement of stone walls, my daughter, than which no two things could be more contrary to the nature of those who dwells in the woods and lanes. I will not deny that the clergyman—and especially the young clergy-woman—had been very good to him; but for which he would probably have run away long before. But what is bred in the bone comes out in the flesh. He does pretty well with the learning, and he bears with the confinement of school, though it is worse than that of the clergy-house. But when a rumour has crept out that he is not the son of the clergyman nor of the clergywoman, and he is taunted with being a gipsy and a vagrant, he lays his bare hands on those nearest to him, my daughter, and comes away on his bare feet."

"How did he find you, Mother?"

"He has no fixed intentions beyond running away, my daughter; but as he is sitting in a hedge to bandage one of his feet with his handkerchief, he sees our patteran, and he goes on, keeping it by the left, and sees it again, and so follows it, and comes home."

"You mean that he came to you?"

"I do, my dear. For home is not a house that never moves from one place, built of stone or brick, and with a front door for the genteel and a back door for the common people. If it was so, prisons would be homes. But home, my daughter, is

Juliana Horatia Ewing

where persons is whom you belongs to, and it may be under a hedge to-day and in a fair to-morrow."

"Mother," said Sybil, "what did you do about the ten pounds?"

"I will tell you, my daughter. I was obliged to wait longer than was agreeable to me before proceeding to that neighbourhood, for the police was searching everywhere, and it would be wearisome to relate to you with what difficulty Christian was concealed. My plans had been long made, as you know.

"Clergyfolk, my daughter, with a tediousness of jaw which makes them as oppressive to listen long to as houses is to rest long in, has their good points like other persons; they shows kindness to those who are in trouble, and they spends their money very freely on the poor. This is well known, even by those who has no liking for parsons, and I have more than once observed that persons who goes straight to the public-house when they has money in their pockets, goes straight to the parson when their pockets is empty.

"It is also well known, my daughter, that when the clergyman collects money after speaking in his church, he doesn't take it for his own use, as is the custom with other people, such as Punch and Judy men, or singers, or fortune tellers; at the same time he is as pleased with a good collection as if it were for his own use; and if some rich person contributes a sovereign for the sick and poor, it is to him as it would be to you, my daughter, if your hand was crossed with gold by some noble gentleman who had been crossed in love.

"I explain this, my dear, that you may understand how it was that I had planned to pay back the clergy people's ten pounds in church, which would be as good as paying it into their hands, with the advantage of secrecy for myself. On the Saturday I drives into the little market in a donkey-cart with greens, and on Sunday morning I goes to church in a very respectable disguisement, and the sexton puts me in a pew with some women of infirm mind in workhouse dresses, for which, my daughter, I had much to do to restrain myself from knocking him down. But I does; and I behaves myself through the service with the utmost care, following the movements of the genteeler portion of the company, those in the pew with me having no manners at all; one of them standing most of the time and giggling over the pew-back, and another sitting in the corner and weeping into her lap.

"But with the exception of getting up and sitting down, and holding a book open as near to the middle as I could guess, I pays little attention, my daughter, for all my thoughts is taken up with waiting for the collection to begin, and with trying to keep my eyes from the clergywoman's face, which I can see quite clearly, though she is at some distance from me."

"Did she look very wild, Mother, as if she felt beside herself?"

"She looked very bad, my daughter, and grey, which was not with age. I tells you that I tried not to look at her; and by and by the collection begins.

"It seems hours to me, my daughter, whilst the money is chinking and the clergyman is speaking, and the ten pieces of gold is getting so hot in my hands, I fancies they burns me, and still not one of the collecting-men comes near our pew.

"At last, one by one, they begins to go past me and go up to the clergyman who is waiting for them at the upper end, and

Juliana Horatia Ewing

then I perceives that they regards us as too poor to pay our way like the rest, and that the plates will never be put into our pew at all. So when the last but one is going past me, I puts out my hand to beckon him, and the woman that is standing by me bursts out laughing, and the other cries worse than ever, and the collecting-man says, 'Hush! hush!' and goes past and takes the plate with him.

"'A black curse on your insolence!' says I; and then I grips the laughing woman by the arm and whispers, 'If you make that noise again, I'll break your head,' and she sits down and begins to cry like the other.

"There is one more collecting-man, who comes last, and he is the Duke, who lives at the big house.

"The nobility and gentry, my daughter, when they are the real thing, has, like the real Romans, a quickness to catch your meaning, and a politeness of manner which you doesn't meet with among such people as the keeper of a small shop or the master of a workhouse. The Duke was a very old man, with bent shoulders and the slow step of age, and I thinks he did not see or hear very quickly; and when I beckons to him he goes past. But when he is some way past he looks back. And when he sees my hand out, he turns and comes slowly down again, and hands me the plate with as much politeness as if I had been in his own pew, and he says in a low voice, 'I beg your pardon.'

"But when I sees him stumbling back, and knows that in his politeness he will bring me the plate, there comes a fear on me, my daughter, that he may see the ten pieces of gold and think I has stolen them. And then I knows not what I shall do, for the nobility and gentry, though quick and polite in a matter of obliging the poor, such as this one,—when they sits as poknees[C] to administer justice, loses both their good sense and their good manners as completely as any of the police.

"But it comes to me also that being such a real one—such an out-and-outer—his politeness may be so great that he may look another way, rather than peep and pry to see what the poor workhouse-company woman puts into the plate. And I am right, my daughter, for he looks away, and I lays the ten golden sovereigns in the plate, and he gives a little smile and a little bow, and goes slowly and stumblingly to the upper end, where the clergyman is still speaking verses.

"And then, my daughter, my hands, which made the gold sovereigns so hot, turns very hot, and I gets up and goes out of the church with as much respectfulness and quiet as I am able.

"And I tries not to look at her face as I turns to shut the door, but I was unable to keep myself from doing so, and as it looked then I can see it now, my dear, and I know I shall remember it till I die. I thinks somehow that she was praying, though it was not a praying part of the service, and when I looks to the upper end I sees that the eyes of the young clergyman her husband is fixed on her, as mine is.

"And of all the words which he preached that day and the verses he spoke with so much readiness, I could not repeat one to you, my daughter, to save my life, except the words he was saying just then, and they remains in my ears as her face remains before my eyes,—

"'GOD is not unrighteous, that He will forget your work, and labour which proceedeth of love.'"

Juliana Horatia Ewing

CHAPTER VI

"We are all creatures of habit." So my learned uncle, Draen y Coed, who was a Welsh hedgehog, used to say. "Which was why an ancestor of my own, who acted as turnspit in the kitchen of a farmhouse in Yorkshire, quite abandoned the family custom of walking out in the cool of the evening, and declared that he couldn't take two steps in comfort except in a circle, and in front of a kitchen-fire at roasting heat."

Uncle Draen y Coed was right, and I must add that I doubt if, in all his experience, or among the strange traditions of his most eccentric ancestors, he could find an instance of change of habits so unexpected, so complete, I may say so headlong, as when very quiet people, with an almost surly attachment to home, break the bounds of the domestic circle, and take to gadding, gossiping, and excitement.

Perhaps it is because they find that their fellow-creatures are nicer than they have been wont to allow them to be, and that other people's affairs are quite as interesting as their own.

Perhaps—but what is the good of trying to explain infatuations?

Why do we all love valerian? I can only record that, having set up every prickle on our backs against intruders into our wood, we now dreaded nothing more than that our neighbours should forsake us, and wished for nothing better than for fresh arrivals.

In old days, when my excellent partner and I used to take our evening stroll up the field, we were wont to regard it quite as a grievance if a cousin, who lived at the far end of the hedge, came out and caught us and detained us for a gossip. But now I could hardly settle to my midday nap for thinking of the tinker-mother; and as to Mrs. Hedgehog, she almost annoyed me by her anxiety to see Christian. However, curiosity is the foible of her sex, and I accompanied her daily to the encampment without a murmur.

The seven urchins we sent down to the burdocks to pick snails.

It was not many days after that on which we heard the old tinker-mother relate Christian's history, that we were stopped on our way to the corner where we usually concealed ourselves, by hearing strange voices from the winding pathway above us.

"It's a young man," said I.

"It's Christian!" cried Mrs. Hedgehog.

"I feel sure that it is not," said I; "but if you will keep quiet, I will creep a little forward and see."

I am always in the right, as I make a point of reminding Mrs. Hedgehog whenever we dispute; and I was right on this occasion.

The lad who spoke was a young gentleman of about seventeen, and no more like a gipsy than I am. His fair hair was closely cropped, his eyes were quick and bright, his manner was alert and almost anxious, and though he was very slight as well as very young, he carried himself with dignity and some little importance. A lady, much older than himself, was with him, whom he was helping down the path.

"Take care, Gertrude, take care. There is no hurry, and I believe there's no one in the wood but ourselves."

Juliana Horatia Ewing

"The people at the inn told us that there were gipsies in the neighbourhood," said the lady; "and oh, Ted! this is exactly the wood I dreamt of, except the purple and white—"

"Gertrude! What on earth are you after?"

"The flowers, Ted, the flowers in my dream! There they are, a perfect carpet of them. White—oh, how lovely!—and there, on the other side, are the purple ones. What are they, dear? I know you are a good botanist. He always raved about your collection."

"Nonsense, I'm not a botanist. Several other fellows went in for it when the prize was offered, and all that my collection was good for was his doing. I never did see any one arrange flowers as he did, I must say. Every specimen was pressed so as somehow to keep its own way of growing. And when I did them, a columbine looked as stiff as a dog-daisy. I never could keep any character in them. Watson—the fellow who drew so well—made vignettes on the blank pages to lots of the specimens—'Likely Habitats' we called them. He used to sit with his paint-box in my window, and Christian used to sit outside the window, on the edge, dangling his legs, and describing scenes out of his head for Watson to draw. Watson used to say, 'I wish I could paint with my brush as that fellow paints with his tongue'—and when the vignettes were admired, I've heard him say, in his dry way, 'I copied them from Christian's paintings;' and the fellows used to stare, for you know he couldn't draw a line. And when—But I say, Gertrude, for Heaven's sake, don't devour everything I say with those great pitiful eyes of yours. I am a regular brute to talk about him."

"No, Ted, no. It makes me so happy to hear you, and to know that you know how good he really was, and how much he must have been aggravated before—"

"For goodness' sake, don't cry. Christian was a very good fellow, a capital fellow. I never thought I could have got on so well with any one who was—I mean who wasn't—well, of course I mean who was really a gipsy. I don't blame him a bit for resenting being bullied about his parents. I only blame myself for not looking better after him. But you know that well enough—you know it's because I never can forgive myself for having managed so badly when you put him in my care, that I am backing you through this mad expedition, though I don't approve of it one bit, and though I know John will blame me awfully."

("It's the clergywoman," whispered Mrs. Hedgehog excitedly, "and I must and will see her."

When it comes to this with Mrs. Hedgehog's sex, there is nothing for it but to let the dear creatures have their own way, and take the consequences. She pushed her nose straight through the lower branches of an arbutus in which we were concealed, and I myself managed to get a nearer sight of our new neighbours.

As we crept forward, the clergywoman got up from where she was kneeling amongst the flowers, and laid her hand on the young gentleman's arm. I noticed it because I had never seen such a white hand before; Sybil's paws were nearly as dark as my own.)

"John will blame no one if we find Christian," she said. "You are very, very good, Cousin Ted, to come with me and help me when you do not believe in my dream. But you must say it is odd about the flowers. And you haven't told me yet what they are."

"It is the bulbous-rooted fumitory," said the young man, pulling a piece at random in the reckless way in which men

Juliana Horatia Ewing

do disfigure forest flower-beds. "It isn't strictly indigenous, but it is naturalized in many places, and you must have seen it before, though you fancy you haven't."

"I have seen it once before," she said earnestly—"all in delicate glaucous-green masses, studded with purple and white, like these; but it was in my dream. I never saw it otherwise, though I know you don't believe me."

"Dear Gertrude, I'll believe anything you like to tell me, if you'll come home. I'm sure I have done very wrong. You know I'm always hard up, but I declare I'd give a hundred pounds if you'd come home with me at once. I don't believe there's a gipsy within—"

"Good-day, my pretty young gentleman. Let the poor gipsy girl tell you your fortune."

He turned round and saw Sybil standing at his elbow, her eyes flashing and her white teeth gleaming in a broad smile. He stood speechless in sudden surprise; but the clergy-woman, who was not surprised, came forward with her white hands stretched so expressively towards Sybil's brown ones, that the gipsy girl all but took them in her own.

"Please kindly tell me—do you know anything of a young gipsy, named Christian?"

The clergywoman spoke with such vehemence that Sybil answered directly, "I know his grandmother"—and then suddenly stopped herself.

But as she spoke, she had turned her head with an expressive gesture in the direction of the encampment, and without waiting for more, the clergywoman ran down the path, calling on her cousin to follow her.

CHAPTER VII

My ancestor's artifice was very successful when the race was run on two sides of a hedge, backwards and forwards; but if a louis d'or and a bottle of brandy had depended on my reaching the tinker-mother before the clergywoman, I should have lost the wager. We hurried after her, however, as fast as we were able, keeping well under the brushwood.

When we could see our neighbours again, the tinker-mother was standing up, and speaking hurriedly, with a wild look in her eyes.

"Let me be, Sybil Stanley, and let me speak. I says again, what has fine folk to do with coming and worriting us in our wood? If I did sell him, I sold him fair—and if I got him back, I bought him back fair. Aye my delicate gentlewoman, you may look at me, but I did!

"Five years, five years of wind and weather, and hard days and lonely nights:—

"Five years of food your men would chuck to the pigs, and of clothes your maids would think scorn to scour in:—

"Five years—but I scraped it together, and *then* they baulked me. You shuts the door in the poor tinker-woman's face; you gives the words of warning to the police.

"Five more years—it was five more, wasn't it, my daughter? —Sometimes I fancies I makes a mistake and overcounts. But, *he'll* know. Christian, my dear! Christian, I say!"

"Sit down, Mother, sit down," said the gipsy girl; and the old woman sat down, but she went on muttering,—

"I will speak! What has they to do, I say, to ask me where he has gone to? A fine place for the fine gentleman they made of him. What has such as them to say to it, if I couldn't keep him when I got him—that they comes to taunt me and my grey hairs?"

She wrung her grey locks with a passionate gesture as she spoke, and then dropped her elbows on her knees and her head upon her hands.

The clergywoman had been standing very still, with her two white hands folded before her, and her eyes, that had dark circles round them which made them look large, fixed upon the tinker-mother, as she muttered; but when she ceased muttering the clergywoman unlocked her hands, and with one movement took off her hat. Her hair was smoothly drawn over the roundness of her head, and gathered in a knot at the back of her neck, and the brown of it was all streaked with grey. She threw her hat on to the grass, and moving swiftly to the old woman's side, she knelt by her, as we had seen Sybil kneel, speaking very clearly, and, touching the tinker-mother's hand.

"Christian's grandmother—you are his grandmother, are you not?—you must be much, much older than me, but look at *my* hair. Am I likely to taunt any one with having grown grey or with being miserable? It takes a good deal of pain, good mother, to make young hair as white as mine."

"So it should," muttered the old woman, "so it should. It is a plaguy world, I say, as it is; but it would be plaguy past any bearing for the poor, if them that has everything could do just as they likes and never feel no aches nor pains afterwards. And there's a many fine gentlefolk thinks they can, till they feels the difference.

"'What's ten pound to me?' says you. 'I wants the pretty baby with the dark eyes and the long lashes,' says you."

"'Them it belongs to is poor, they'd sell anything,' says you."

"'I wants a son,' you says; 'and having the advantages of gold and silver, I can buy one.'"

"You calls him by a name of your own choosing, and puts your own name at the end of that. His hands are something dark for the son of such a delicate white lady-mother, but they can be covered with the kid gloves of gentility."

"You buys fine clothes for him, and nurses and tutors and schools for him."

"You teaches him the speech of gentlefolk, and the airs of gentlefolk, and the learning of gentlefolk."

"You crams his head with religion, which is a thing I doesn't hold with, and with holy words, which I thinks brings ill-luck."

"You has the advantages of silver and gold, to make a fine gentleman of him, but the blood that flies to his face when he hears the words of insult is gipsy blood, and he comes back to the woods where he was born."

"Let me be, my daughter, I say I will speak—(Heaven keep my head cool!)—it's good for such as them to hear the truth once in a way. She's a dainty fine lady, and she taught him many fine things, besides religion, which I sets my face against. Tell her she took mighty good care of him—Ha! ha! the old tinker-woman had only one chance of teaching him anything—*but she taught him the patteran*!"

Juliana Horatia Ewing

The clergywoman had never moved, except that when the tinker-mother shook off her hand she locked her white fingers in front of her as before, and her eyes wandered from the old woman's face, and looked beyond it, as if she were doing what I have often done, and counting the bits of blue sky which show through the oak-leaves before they grow thick. But she must have been paying attention all the same, for she spoke very earnestly.

"Good mother, listen to me. If I bought him, you sold him. Perhaps I did wrong to tempt you—perhaps I did wrong to hope to buy for myself what GOD was not pleased to give me. I was very young, and one makes many mistakes when one is young. I thought I was childless and unhappy, but I know now that only those are childless who have had children and lost them.

"Do you know that in all the years my son was with me, I do not think there was a day when I did not think of you? I used to wonder if you regretted him, and I lived in dread of your getting him back; and when he ran away, I knew you had. I never agreed with the lawyer's plans—my husband will tell you so—I always wanted to find you to speak to you myself. I knew what you must feel, and I thought I should like you to know that I knew it.

"Night after night I lay awake and thought what I would say to you when we met. I thought I would tell you that I could quite understand that our ways might become irksome to Christian, if he inherited a love for outdoor life, and for moving from place to place. I thought I would say that perhaps I was wrong ever to have taken him away from his own people; but as it was done and could not be undone, we might perhaps make the best of it together. I hope you understand me, though you say nothing? You see, if he is a gipsy at heart, he has also been brought up to many comforts you cannot give him, and with the habits and ideas of a gentleman. You are too clever, and too fond of him, to mind my speaking plainly. Now there are things which a gentleman might do if he had the money, which would satisfy his love of roving as well. Many rich gentlemen dislike the confinement of houses and domestic ways as much as Christian, and they leave their fine homes to travel among dangers and discomforts. I could find the money for Christian to do this by and by. If he likes a wandering life, he can live it easily so—only he would be able to wander hundreds of miles where you wander one, and to sleep under other skies and among new flowers, and in forests to which such woods as these are shrubberies. He need not fall into any of the bad ways to which you know people are tempted by being poor. I have thought of it all, night after night, and longed to be able to tell you about it. He might become a famous traveller, you know; he is very clever and very fond of books of adventure. This young gentleman will tell you so. How proud we should both be of him! That is what I have thought might be if you did not hide him from me, and I did not keep him from you.

"And as to religion—dear good mother, listen to me. Look at me—see if religion has been a fashion or a plaything to *me*. If it had not stood by me when my heart was as heavy as yours, what profit should I have in it?

"Christian's grandmother—you are his grandmother, I know, and have the better right to him—if you cannot agree to my plans—if you won't let me help you about him—if you hide him from me, and I must live out my life and never see his dear face again—spare me the hope of seeing it when this life is over.

"If I did my best for your grandson—and you know I did—oh! for the love of Christ, our only Refuge, do not stand between him and the Father of us all!

"If you have felt what he must suffer if he is poor, and if you know so well how little it makes sure of happiness to be rich—if in a long life you have found out how hard it is to be good, and how rare it is to be happy—if you know what it is to love and lose, to hope and to be disappointed in one's hoping—let him be religious, good mother!

"If you care for Christian, leave him the only strength that is strong enough to hold us back from sin, and to do instead of joy."

The tinker-mother lifted her head; but before she could say a word, the young gentleman burst into indignant speech.

"Gertrude, I can bear it no longer. Not even for you, not even for the chance of getting Christian back. It's empty swagger to say that I wish to GOD I'd the chance of giving my life to get him back for you. But you must come home now. I've bitten my lip through in holding my tongue, but I won't see you kneel another minute at the feet of that sulky old gipsy hag."

Whilst he was speaking the tinker-mother had risen to her feet, and when she stood quite upright she was much taller than I had thought. The young gentleman had moved to take his cousin by the hand, but the old woman waved him back.

"Stay where you are, young gentleman," she said. "This is no matter for boys to mix and meddle in. Sybil, my daughter—Sybil, I say! Come and stand near me, for I gets confused at times, and I fears I may not explain myself to the noble gentlewoman with all the respect that I could wish. She says a great deal that is very true, my daughter, and she has no vulgar insolence in her manners of speaking. I thinks I shall let her do as she says, if we can get Christian out, which perhaps, if she is cousin to any of the justiciary, she may be able to do.

"The poor tinker-folk returns you the deepest of obligations, my gentle lady. If she'll let me see him when I wants to, it will be best, my daughter; for I thinks I am failing, and I shouldn't like to leave him with George and that drunken slut.

"I thinks I am failing, I say. Trouble and age and the lone company of your own thoughts, my noble gentlewoman, has a tendency to confuse you, though I was always highly esteemed for the facility of my speech, especially in the telling of fortunes.

"Let the poor gipsy look into your white hand, my pretty lady. The lines of life are somewhat broken with trouble, but they joins in peace. There's a dark young gentleman with a great influence on your happiness, and I sees grandchildren gathered at your knees.

"What did the lady snatch away her hand for, my daughter? I means no offence. She shall have Christian. I have told her so. Tell him to get ready and go before his father gets back. He's a bad 'un is my son George, and I knows now that she was far too good for him.

"Come a little nearer, my dear, that I may touch you. I sees your face so often, when I knows you can't be there, that it pleases me to be able to feel you. I was afraid you bore me ill-will for selling Christian; but I bought him back, my dear, I bought him back. Take him away with you, my dear, for I am failing, and I shouldn't like to leave him with George. Your eyes looks very hollow and your hair is grey. Not, that I begrudges your making so much of my son, but he treats

Juliana Horatia Ewing

you ill, he treats you very ill. Don't cry, my dear, it comes to an end at last, though I thinks sometimes that all the men in the world put together is not worth the love we wastes upon one. You hear what I say, Sybil? And that rascal, Black Basil, is the worst of a bad lot."

"Hold your jaw, Mother," said Sybil sharply; and she added, "Be pleased to excuse her, my lady: she is old and gets confused at times, and she thinks you are Christian's mother, who is dead."

The old woman was bursting out again, when Sybil raised her hand, and we all pricked our ears at a sound of noisy quarrelling that came nearer.

"It's George and his wife," said Sybil. "Mother, the gentle-folks had better go. I'll go to the inn afterwards, and tell them about Christian. Take the lady away, sir. Come, Mother, come!"

I've a horror of gipsy men, and even before our neighbours had dispersed I hustled away with Mrs. Hedgehog into the bushes.

CHAPTER VIII

Good Mrs. Hedgehog hurt one of her feet slightly in our hurried retreat, and next day was obliged to rest it; but as our curiosity was more on the alert than ever, I went down in the afternoon to the tinker camp.

The old woman was sitting in her usual position, and she seemed to have recovered herself. Sybil was leaning back against a tree opposite; she wore a hat and shawl, and looked almost as wild as the tinker-mother had looked the day before. She seemed to have been at the inn with the clergywoman, and was telling the tinker-mother the result.

"You told her he had got two years, my daughter? Does she say she will get him out?"

"She says she has no more power to do it than yourself, Mother—and the young gentleman says the same—unless—unless it was made known that Christian was innocent."

"Two years," moaned the old woman. "Is she sure we couldn't buy him out, my dear? Two years—oh! Christian, my child, I shall never live to see you again!"

She sobbed for a minute, and then raising her hand suddenly above her head, she cried, "A curse on Black—" but Sybil seized her by the wrist so suddenly, that it checked her words.

"Don't curse him, Mother," said the gipsy girl, "and I'll—I'll see what I can do. I meant to, and I've come to say good-bye. I've brought a packet of tea for you; see that you keep it to yourself. Good-bye, Mother."

Juliana Horatia Ewing

"Good-evening, my daughter."

"I said good-bye. You don't hold with religion, do you?"

"I does not, so far, my daughter; though I think the young clergywoman speaks very convincingly about it."

"Don't you think that there may be a better world, Mother, for them that tries to do right, though things goes against them here?"

"I think there might very easily be a better world, my dear, but I never was instructed about it."

"You don't believe in prayers, do you, Mother?"

"That I does not, my daughter. Christian said lots of 'em, and you sees what it comes to."

"It's not unlucky to say 'GOD bless you,' is it, Mother? I wanted you to say it before I go."

"No, my daughter, I doesn't object to that, for I regards it as an old-fashioned compliment, more in the nature of good manners than of holy words."

"GOD bless you, Mother."

"GOD bless you, my daughter."

Sybil turned round and walked steadily away. The last glimpse I had of her was when she turned once more, and put the hair from her face to look at the old woman: but the tinker-mother did not see her, for she was muttering with her head upon her hands.

*   *   *   *   *

It was a remarkable summer—that summer when I had seven, and when we took so much interest in our neighbours.

I make a point of never disturbing myself about the events of by-gone seasons. At the same time, to rear a family of seven urchins is not a thing done by hedgehog-parents every year, and the careers of that family are very clearly impressed upon my memory.

Number one came to a sad end.

What on the face of the wood made him think of pheasants' eggs, I cannot conceive. I'm sure I never said anything about them! It was whilst he was scrambling along the edge of the covert, that he met the Fox, and very properly rolled himself into a ball. The Fox's nose was as long as his own, and he rolled my poor son over and over with it, till he rolled him into the stream. The young urchins swim like fishes, but just as he was scrambling to shore, the Fox caught him by the waistcoat and killed him. I do hate slyness!

Numbers two and three were flitted. I told them so, but young people will go their own way. They had excellent victuals.

Number four (my eldest daughter) settled very comfortably in life, and had a family of three. She might have sent them down to the burdocks to pick snails quite well, but she would take them out walking with her instead. They were picked up (all four of them) by two long-legged Irish boys, who put them into a basket and took them home. I do not think the young gentlemen meant any harm, for they provided plenty of food, and took them to bed with them. They set my daughter at liberty next day, and she spoke very handsomely

Juliana Horatia Ewing

of the young gentlemen, and said they had cured the skins with saltpetre, and were stuffing them when she left. But the subject was always an awkward one.

Number five is still living. He is the best hand at a fight with a snake that I know.

Numbers six and seven went to Covent Garden in a hamper. They say black-beetles are excellent eating.

The whole seven had a narrow escape with their lives just after Sybil left us. They over-ate themselves on snails, and Mrs. Hedgehog had to stay at home and nurse them. I kept my eye on our neighbours and brought her the news.

"Christian has come home," I said, one day. "The Queen has given him a pardon."

"Then he *did* take the pheasants' eggs?" said Mrs. Hedgehog.

"Certainly not," said I. "In the first place it wasn't eggs, and in the second place it was Black Basil who took whatever it was, and he has confessed to it."

"Then if Christian didn't do it, how is it that he has been forgiven?" said Mrs. Hedgehog.

"I can't tell you," said I; "but so it is. And he is at this moment with the clergywoman and the tinker-mother."

"Where is Sybil?" asked Mrs. Hedgehog.

I did not know then, and I am not very clear about her now. I never saw her again, but either I heard that she had married Black Basil, and that they had gone across the water to some country where the woods are bigger than they are here, or I have dreamt it in one of my winter naps.

I am inclined to think it must be true, because I always regarded Sybil as somewhat proud and unsociable, and I think she would like a big wood and very few neighbours.

But really when one sleeps for several months at a stretch it is not very easy to be accurate about one's dreams.

FOOTNOTES:

Footnote B: *Patteran* = the gipsy "trail."

Footnote C: "Poknees," gipsy word for magistrate.

TOOTS AND BOOTS

*   *   *   *   *

CHAPTER I

My name is Toots. Why, I have not the slightest idea. But I suppose very few people—cats or otherwise—are consulted about their own names. If they were, these would perhaps be, as a rule, more appropriate.

What qualities of mind or body my name was supposed to illustrate, I have not to this hour a notion. I distinctly remember the stage of my kittenhood, when I thought that Toots was the English for cream.

"Toots! Toots!" my young mistress used to say, in the most suggestive tones, creeping after me as I would creep after a mouse, with a saucerful of that delicious liquid in her hand.

"Toots is first-rate stuff," I used to think, and I purred accordingly, for I never was an ungrateful cat.

This was in the dining-room, and in the morning. Later in the day, "Toots" was served in the drawing-room. It was between these two periods, I remember, that one day I found myself in the larder. Why I went there, puzzled me at the time; for if there is anything I hate it is a chill, and there was a horrid draught through a window pierced with tiny holes, which seemed to let in a separate blast for every hair of one's fur. I followed the cook, it is true; but I did not follow the cook as a rule—not, for instance, when she went out to the coal-hole in the yard. I had slipped in under her dress. I was behind the potato-tub when she went out, shutting the door after her. For some mysterious reason I felt on the tip-claw of expectation. My nose twitched with agreeable sensations. An inward voice seemed to murmur, *Toots*! Regardless of the draughts, I sprang on to the shelf close under the window. And there was such a dish of cream! The saucers in which one got it at breakfast did not hold a twentieth part of what this brimming pan contained. As to the five o'clock china, in which visitors give you a tepid teaspoonful, with bits of old tea-leaves in it—I grinned at the thought as I drew in tongueful after tongueful of the thick yellow cream.

At this moment I heard my young mistress's voice in the distant passages.

"Toots, Toots!" said she.

"I've got plenty," purred I, lifting my head to speak, by a great effort.

"Toots, Toots!" she miowed on, for she wasn't much quicker-witted than the rest of her race.

"No, thank you," thought I; "and if you want five o'clock toots for yourself, I advise you to come here for it." I thought this, but speak I really could not—I was too busy lapping.

It was delicious stuff! But when the dish was about three-parts empty, I began to feel as if I had had a good deal, and

Juliana Horatia Ewing

to wish I had more appetite for the rest. "It's a shame to leave it, though," I thought, "when a few more laps will empty the dish." For I come of an ancient and rough-tongued cat family, who always lick their platters clean. So I set to work again, though the draught was most annoying, and froze the cream to butter on my whiskers.

I was polishing the glazed earthenware with the family skill, when I became conscious that the house was resounding to the cry of "Toots!"

"Toots, Toots!" squeaked the housemaid, in the servants' hall.

"Toots, Toots!" growled the elderly butler, in the pantry.

"Toots, Toots, cock-a-Toots!" yelled that intolerable creature, the Macaw.

"Toots, Toots!" snapped the cook.

"Miow," said I; for I had finished the cream, and could speak now, though I confess I did not feel equal to any great exertion.

The cook opened the door. She found me—she did not find the cream, which she had left in the dish ready for whipping.

Perhaps it was because she had no cream to whip, that she tried to whip me. Certainly, during the next half-hour, I had reason to be much confused as to the meaning of the word "Toots." In the soft voice of my mistress it had always seemed to me to mean cream; now it seemed to mean kicks, blows, flapping dish-cloths, wash-leathers and dusters, pokers, carpet brooms, and every instrument of torture with which a poor cat could be chased from garret to cellar. I am pretty nimble, and though I never felt less disposed for violent exercise, I flatter myself I led them a good dance before, by a sudden impulse of affectionate trustfulness, I sprang straight into my mistress's arms for shelter.

"You must beat him, miss," gasped the cook, "or there'll never be no bearing him in the house. Every drop of that lovely cream gone, and half the sweets for the ball supper throwed completely out of calculation!"

"Naughty Toots, naughty Toots, naughty Toots!" cried the young lady, and with every "Toots" she gave me a slap; but as her paws had no claws in them, I was more offended than hurt.

This was my first lesson in honesty, and it was also the beginning of that train of reasoning in my own mind, by which I came to understand that when people called "Toots" they meant me. And as—to do them justice—they generally called me with some kind intention, I made a point of responding to my name.

Indeed, they were so kind to me, and my position was such a very comfortable one, that when a lean tabby called one day for a charitable subscription, and begged me to contribute a few spare partridge bones to a fund for the support of starving cats in the neighbourhood, who had been deserted by families leaving town, I said that really such cases were not much in my line. There is a great deal of imposition about—perhaps the cats had stolen the cream, and hadn't left off stealing it when they were chased by the family. I doubted if families where the cats deserved respect and consideration ever did leave town. One has so many calls, if one once begins to subscribe to things; and I am particularly fond of partridge.

Juliana Horatia Ewing

But when, a few months later, the very words which the lean tabby had spoken passed between the butler and the cook in reference to our own household, and I learnt that "the family" were going "to leave town," I felt a pang of conscience, and wished I had subscribed the merry thought, or even the breast-bone—there was very little on it—to the Deserted Cats' Fund.

But it was my young mistress who told me (with regrets and caresses, which in the circumstances were mere mockery) that I was to be left behind.

I have a particularly placid temper, and can adapt myself pretty comfortably to the ups and downs of life; but this news made my tail stand on end.

"Poor dear Toots!" said my mistress, kissing my nose, and tickling me gently under the ear, as if she were saying the prettiest things possible. "I am *so* sorry! I don't know *what* we are to do with you! But we are going abroad, and we *can't* take you, you dear old thing! We've such heaps of luggage, and such lots of servants, and no end of things that *must* go! But I *can't bear to think* of you left behind!"

"No," said I indignantly; "that's just it, and the people at number ten, and number fourteen, and number twenty-five, couldn't bear to think what would become of their cats, so they went away and didn't think about it. They couldn't bear to see them die, so they didn't give them a dose of quick poison, but left them to die of starvation, when they weren't there to see. You're a heartless, selfish race, you human beings, and I suspect that Mrs. Tabby is not the only shabby-looking, true-hearted soul, who has to pester people for subscriptions to patch up the dreary end of existence for deserted pets, when caressing days are over. Fuff!"

And I jumped straight out of her arms, and whisked through the dining-room window. For some time I strolled thoughtfully along the top of the area railings. I rather hoped I might see Mrs. Tabby. I wondered how her subscription list was getting on. I felt all the difference between a lady's interest in a Reduced Gentlewomen's Benevolent Institution or a Poor Annuitants' Home, when she is well and wealthy, and the same lady's interest when some turn of Misfortune's wheel has left her "dependent on her own exertions." It seemed that I was to be left dependent on my own exertions—and my thoughts turned naturally to Mrs. Tabby and the Deserted Cats' Fund.

But not a sign of the good creature! At this moment a hansom cab rattled up, and a gentleman got out and rang our front-door bell. As he got out of the cab, I jumped down from the railings, and rubbed against his legs—he had very long legs.

"Halloa, Toots! is that you?" said he in a kindly voice, which had always had attractions for me, and which in my present mood was particularly grateful. His hat was set well on the back of his head, and I could clearly see the friendly expression of his countenance. Suddenly he tilted it over his nose, which I have observed that he is apt to do when struck by a new idea. "Toots!" said he abruptly, "what are they going to do with you?"

Blessings on this kind of friend! say I; the friend who will encumber himself with the responsibility of thinking what's to become of you, when you are down in the world. Those tender-hearted souls who can't bear to think of your misfortunes are a much more numerous part of one's acquaintance.

A ray of hope began to dawn upon me. Perhaps a new and an even more luxurious home was to be offered for my acceptance. In what foolish panic had I begun to identify myself with the needy classes of society? A cat of my stripes and style! Once more I thought of benevolent institutions from a patronizing point of view. But I would be a patron, and a generous one. The shock *had* done so much! And the next time Mrs. Tabby called I would *pick out a lot of my best bones for the Fund.*

Meanwhile, I went back to the railings, and from these took a flying leap, and perched myself on the gentleman's shoulder. I could hardly have managed it from the ground, he had such very long legs.

I think, by the bye, that I have mentioned this before. I do not wish to repeat myself, or to dwell on my grievance, though, if his legs had been shorter, his riding-boots would not have been so long, and I might at this moment know what became of—but I must not forestall my story.

I jumped on to the gentleman's shoulder. In doing so, I knocked his hat over one eye. But I have seen it so since then, and he made no complaint. The man-servant opened the door, and we went into the house together.

CHAPTER II

I flatter myself that my head is not remarkable for size and beauty alone. I am a cat of mind, and I made it up at once as to the course of conduct to pursue.

I am also a cat with some powers of observation, and I have observed that two things go a long way with men—flattery and persistence. Also that the difficulty of coaxing them is not in direct proportion to their size—rather the reverse. Another thing that I have observed is, that if you want to be well-treated, or have a favour to ask, it is a great thing to have a good coat on your back in good order.

How many a human being has sleeked the rich softness of my magnificent tiger skin, and then said, in perfect good faith, "How Toots enjoys being stroked!"

"How you enjoy the feel of my fur, you mean," I am tempted to say. But I do not say it. It doesn't do to disturb the self-complacency of people who have the control of the milk-jug.

Having made up my mind to coax the gentleman into adopting me, I devoted myself entirely to him for the evening, and ignored the rest of the party, as serenely as a cat knows how. Again and again did he put me down with firm, but not ungentle hands, saying—"Go down, Toots," and pick stray hairs in a fidgety manner off his dress-trousers; and again and again did I return to his shoulder (where he couldn't see the hairs) and purr in his ear, and rub my long whiskers against his short ones.

But it was not till he was comfortably established in an arm-chair by the drawing-room fire, round which the rest of the family were also seated, that the charm began to work.

Juliana Horatia Ewing

"How devoted Toots is to you!" purred the ladies, after an ineffectual effort on my part to share the arm-chair.

"You're a very foolish Toots," said the gentleman. (I was back on his shoulder by this time.)

"Toots, you've deserted me," said my young mistress. "I'm quite jealous," she added.

"Toots, you brute!" cried the gentleman, seizing me in both hands. "Where's your good taste, and your gratitude? Go to your mistress, sir," and he threw me into her lap. But I sprang back to his shoulder with one leap.

"It's really most extraordinary," said one lady.

"And Toots never goes to strangers as a rule," added my mistress.

Everybody is proud of being *exceptionally* favoured. It was this last stroke, I am convinced, that rubbed him the right way. A gratified blandness pervaded his countenance. He made no further attempts to dislodge me, and I settled myself into the angles of his shoulder and affected to go to sleep.

"What are you going to do with him?" he asked, crossing one long leg over the other with a convulsive abruptness very trying to my balance, and to the strength of the arm-chair.

Both the ladies began to mew. They were *so* sorry to leave me behind, but it was *quite* impossible to take me. They couldn't bear to think of my being unhappy, and didn't know where in the world to find me a home.

"I wish *you* would take him!" said my mistress.

I listened breathlessly for the gentleman's reply.

"Pets are not in the least in my line," he said. "I am a bachelor, you know, of very tidy habits. I dislike trouble, and have a rooted objection to encumbrances."

"We hear you have a pet mouse, though," said my mistress. He laughed awkwardly.

"My dear young lady, I never said that my practice always squared with my principles. Helpless and troublesome creatures have sometimes an insinuating way with them, which forms an additional reason for avoiding them, especially if one is weak-minded. And—"

"And you *have* a pet mouse?"

He sat suddenly upright with another jerk, which nearly shot me into the fire-place, and said,

"I'll tell you about it, for upon my word I wish you could see the little beggar. It was one afternoon when I came in from riding, that I found a mouse sitting on the fender. I could only see his back, with the tail twitching, and I noticed that a piece had been bitten out of his left ear. The little wretch must have heard me quite well, but he sat on as if the place belonged to him."

"'You're pretty cool!' I said; and being rather the reverse myself, I threw the Queen's Regulations at him, and he disappeared. But it bothered me, for I hate mice in one's quarters. You never know what mischief they mayn't be doing. You put valuable papers carefully away, and the next time you go to the cupboard, they are reduced to shreds. The little brutes take the lining of your slippers to line their nests. They keep you awake at night—in short, they're detestable.

Juliana Horatia Ewing

But I am not fond of killing things myself, though I've a sort of a conscience about knowing how it's done. I don't like leaving necessary executions to servants. As to mice, you know—poisoning is out of the question, on sanitary grounds. 'Catch-'em-alive' traps are like a policeman who catches a pickpocket—all the trouble of the prosecution is to come; and as to the traps with springs and spikes—my man set one in my bedroom once, and in the middle of the night the mouse was caught. For nearly an hour I doubt if I was much the happier of the two. Every moment I thought the poor wretch would stop screaming, for I had ordered the trap in the belief that death was instantaneous. At last I jumped up, and put the whole concern into my tub and held it under water. The poor beast was dead in six seconds. A catch-'em-alive trap and a tub of water is the most merciful death, I fancy; but I am rather in favour of letting one animal kill another. It seems more natural, and *fairer*. They have a run for their lives, so to speak."

"And who did you get to kill your mouse?"

"Well, I know a youngster who has a terrier. They are a perfect pair. As like as two peas, and equally keen about sport—they would go twenty miles to chase a bluebottle round an attic, sooner than not hunt something. So I told him there was a mouse *de trop* in my rooms, and he promised to bring Nipper next morning. I was going out hunting myself."

"The meet was early, and my man got breakfast at seven o'clock for me in my own quarters; and the first thing I saw when I came out of my bedroom was the mouse sitting on the edge of my Indian silver sugar-basin. I knew him again by his ear. And there he sat all breakfast-time, twitching his tail, and nibbling little bits of sugar, and watching me with such a pair of eyes! Have you ever seen a mouse's eyes close? Upon my word, they are wonderfully beautiful, and it's uncommonly difficult to hurt a creature with fine eyes. I didn't touch it, and as I was going out I looked back, and *the mouse was looking after me*. I was a fool for looking back, for I can't stand a pitiful expression in man or beast, and it put an end to Nipper's sport, and left me with a mouse in my quarters—a thing I hate. I didn't like to say I'd changed my mind about killing the mouse, but I wrote to Nipper's master, and said I wouldn't trouble him to come up for such a trifling matter."

"So the mouse was safe?"

"Well, *I* thought so. But the young fellow (who is very good-natured) wrote back to say it was no trouble whatever, and the letter lay on my mantel-piece till I came home and found that he and Nipper had broken a chair-leg, and two china plates."

"*Did* they kill the mouse?"

"Well, no. But I nearly killed Nipper in saving him; and the little rascal has lived with me ever since."

The ladies seemed highly delighted with this anecdote, but, for my own part, I felt feverish to the tips of my claws, as I thought of the miserable creature who had usurped the place I wished to fill, and who might be the means of my having to fall back after all on the Deserted Cats' Fund. What bungling puss had had him under her paws, and allowed him to escape with a torn ear and the wariness of experience? Let me but once catch sight of that twitching tail!—

At this moment the gentleman got up, stretched his long—

But I will *not* allude to them! It annoys me as much as the thought of that bungling cat, or of Nipper's baulked attempt.

Juliana Horatia Ewing

He put up his hands and lifted me from his shoulder, and my heart sank as he said, "If I am to catch my train, I fear I must say good-bye."

I believe that, in this hopeless crisis, my fur as usual was in my favour. He rubbed his cheek against mine before putting me down, and then said, "And you've not told me, after all, where poor Toots is really going."

"We have not found a home for him yet, I assure you," said my mistress. "Our washerwoman wants him, and she is a most kind-hearted and respectable person, but she has got nine children, and—"

"Nine children!" ejaculated my friend, "My poor Toots, there will not be an inch of that magnificent tail of yours left at the end of a week. What cruelty to animals! Upon my word, I'd almost rather take Toots myself, than think of him with a washerwoman and nine children. Eh, Toots! would you like to come?"

I was on the carpet, rubbing against his—yes, long or short, they were *his*, and he was kind to me!—rubbing, I say, against his legs. I could get no impetus for a spring, but I scrambled straight up him as one would scramble up a tree (my grandmother was a bird-catcher of the first talent, and I inherit her claws), and uttered one pitiful mew.

The gentleman gave a short laugh, and took me into his arms.

"Oh, *how* good of you! Jones shall get a hamper," cried the ladies. But he shook his head.

"Three of the fourteen parcels I've got to pick up at the station are hampers. I wouldn't have another on my mind for a fortune. If Toots comes at all, he must come like a Christian and look after himself."

I will not dwell on our departure. It was a sadly flurried one, for a cat of my temperament. The ladies saw us off, and as my young mistress covered me with farewell kisses, I felt an unquestionable pang of regret. But one has to repress one's affections, and consider one's prospects in life, if one does not want to come upon the Deserted Cats' Fund!

My master put his hat on the back of his head on the steps, and knocked it off in shouting through a hole in the roof of the cab that we were to drive like the wind, as we were late. At the last moment several things were thrown in after us. A parcel of books he had lent the young lady, and a pair of boots he had left behind on some former occasion. The books were very neatly packed, and addressed, but the boots came "like Christians, and looked after themselves." And through all, I clung fast, and blessed the inherited vigour of my grandmother's claws.

At the parcels office, I certainly risked nine lives among the fourteen parcels which were dragged and pitched, and turned over in every direction; but though he paid me no other attention, my master never forgot to put back a hand to help me when we moved on. Eventually we found ourselves alone in a very comfortable carriage, and I suppose the fourteen packages were safe too, thanks to the desperate struggles of five porters, who went off clutching their paws as if they were satisfied with the result.

After incommoding me for some time by rustling news-papers, and making spasmodic struggles to find a posture that suited him, my master found one at last and fell asleep, and I crept up to the velvet collar of his great-coat and followed his example.

Juliana Horatia Ewing

CHAPTER III

I like living with bachelors. They have comfortable chairs, and keep good fires. They don't put water into the tea-pot: they call the man-servant and send for more tea. They don't give you a table-spoonful of cream, fidgeting and looking round to see if anybody else wants it: one of them turns the jug upside-down into your saucer, and before another can lay hold of it and say, "Halloa! The milk's all gone,"—you have generally had time to lap it up under the table.

I prefer men's outsides, too, to women's in some respects. Why all human beings—since they have no coats of their own, and are obliged to buy them—do not buy handsomely marked furs whilst they are about it, is a puzzle to a cat. As to the miserable stuff ladies cover themselves with in an evening, there is about as much comfort and softness in it as in going to sleep on a duster. Men's coats are nothing to boast of, either to look at or to feel, but they *are* thicker. If you happen to clutch a little with gratification or excitement, your claws don't go through; and they don't squeak like a mouse in a trap and call you treacherous because their own coats are thin.

I was very comfortable in my new home. My master was exceedingly kind to me, and he has a fearless and friendly way of tickling one's toes which is particularly agreeable, and not commonly to be met with.

Yes, my life was even more luxurious than before. It is so still. To eat, drink, and sleep, to keep oneself warm, and in good condition, and to pay proper attention to one's personal appearance; that is all one has to do in a life like mine in bachelors' quarters.

One has unpleasant dreams sometimes. I think my tea is occasionally too strong, though I have learned to prefer it to milk, and my master always gives it to me in his own saucer. If he has friends to tea, they give me some in their saucers. One can't refuse, but I fancy too much tea is injurious to the nerves.

The night before last, I positively dreamed that I was deserted. I fancied that I was chased along a housetop, and fell from the gutter. Down—down—but I woke up on the bear-skin before the fire, as our man-servant was bringing in candles.

It made me wonder how Mrs. Tabby was getting on. I had never done anything further in that matter; but really when one's life goes in a certain groove, and everything one can wish for is provided in abundance, one never seems to have time for these things. It is wonderful how energetic some philanthropic people are. I dare say they like the fuss. (I can't endure fuss!) And Mrs. Tabby's appearance—excellent creature!—would probably make her feel ill-at-ease in bachelor quarters, if we could change places. Her fur is really almost mangy, and she has nothing to speak of in the way of a tail. But she is a worthy soul. And some day, when the Captain and I are going to town without much luggage— or if she should happen to be collecting in the country,—I will certainly *look up a few of my worst bones for the Fund.*

I really hesitate to approach the subject of my one source of discontent. It seems strange that there should be any crook in a lot so smooth as ours. Plenty to eat and drink, handsome coats, no encumbrances, and a temperament naturally inclined—at least, in my case—towards taking life easy. And yet, as I lay stretched full-length down one of my master's knees the other night, before a delicious fire, and after such a saucerful of creamy tea which he could not drink himself—I

Juliana Horatia Ewing

kept waking up with uncomfortable starts, fancying I saw on the edge of the fender—but I will tell the matter in proper order.

I turned round to get my back to it, but I thought of it all the same; and as every hair of my moustaches twitched, with the vexation of my thoughts, I observed that my master was pulling and biting at his, and glaring at the fire as if *he* expected to see—however, I do not trouble myself about the crumples in *his* rose-leaves. He is big enough to take care of himself. My own grievance I will state plainly and at once. It may be a relief to my mind, which I sometimes fear will be unhinged by dwelling on the thought of—but to begin.

It will easily be understood that after my arrival at my new home, I waited anxiously for the appearance of the mouse; but it will hardly be credited by any one who knows me, or who knew my grandmother, that I saw it and *let it escape me*. It was seated on the sugar-basin, just as the Captain had described it. The torn ear, the jerking tail, the bright eyes—all were there.

If this story falls into the paws of any young cat who wishes to avoid the mortifications which have embittered my favoured existence, let me warn him to remember that a creature who has lived on friendly terms with human beings cannot be judged by common rules. Many a mouse's eye as bright as this one had I seen, but hitherto never one that did not paralyze before my own.

He looked at me—I looked at him. His tail jerked—mine responded. Our whiskers twitched—joy filled my brain to intoxication—I crept—I crouched—I sprang—

He was not spell-bound—he did not even run away. With a cool twinkle of that hateful eye, and one twitch of the ragged ear, he just overbalanced the silver sugar-pot and dropped to the ground, the basin and sugar falling on the top of him with a crash which made me start against my will. I think that start just baulked the lightning flash of my second leap, and he was gone—absolutely gone. To add insult to injury, my master ran in from his bedroom and shouted—"Stealing, Toots? confound you, you've knocked down my sugar-pot," and threw both his hair-brushes at me.

I steal?—and, worse still, *I* knock down anything, who have walked among three dozen wine-glasses, on a shelf in the butler's pantry, without making them jingle! But I must be calm, for there is more to tell.

The mouse never returned. It was something, but it was not enough. My pride had been deeply hurt, and it demanded revenge. At last I felt it almost a grievance that I *did* reign supreme in the Captain's quarters, that the mouse did not come back—and let me catch him.

Besides our in-door man, my master had an Irish groom, and the groom had a place (something between a saddle-room and a scullery) where *he* said he "kept what the master required," but where, the master said, Terence kept what was not wanted, and lost what was.

There certainly were, to my knowledge, fifteen empty Day and Martin's blacking-bottles in one corner, for I used occasionally to walk over them to keep my feet in practice, and it was in this room that Terence last had conscious possession of the hunting-breeches which were never seen after the Captain's birthday, when Terence threw the clothes-brush after me, because I would not drink the master's health in whisky, and had to take the cleanest of the shoe brushes to his own coat, which was dusty from lying in the corn-chest.

Juliana Horatia Ewing

But he was a good-natured creature, and now and then, for a change, I followed him into the saddle-room. I am thankful to say I have never caught mice except for amusement, and a cat of daintier tastes does not exist. But one has inherited instincts—and the musty, fusty, mousey smell of the room did excite me a little. Besides, I practised my steps among the blacking-bottles.

I was on the top of the most tottering part of the pile one afternoon, when I saw a pair of bead-like eyes, and—yes, I could swear to it—a torn ear. But before I could spring to the ground they had vanished behind the corn-chest.

This was how it came about that when the Captain's room was cosiest, and he and his friends were kindest, I used to steal away from luxuries which are dear to every fibre of my constitution, and pat hastily down to the dirty hole, where Terence accumulated old rubbish and misused and mislaid valuables—in the wild hope that I might hear, smell, or see the ragged-eared enemy of my peace.

What hours I have wasted, now blinking with sleep, now on the alert at sounds like the revelries of mocking mice.

When I say that I have even risked wet feet, on a damp afternoon, to get there—every cat will understand how wild must have been the infatuation!

I tried to reason myself out of it. "Toots," I would say, "you banished him from your master's room, and you have probably banished him from Terence's. Why pursue the matter farther? So pitiful an object is unworthy of your revenge."

"Very true," I would reply to myself, "but I want a turn in the air. I'll just step down as far as the saddle-room once more, and make myself finally comfortable by looking behind the old barrel. I don't think I went quite round it."

There is no delusion so strong when it besets you, or so complete a failure in its results—as the hope of getting relief from an infatuation by indulging it once more. It grows worse every time.

One day I was stealing away as usual, when I caught my master's eye with a peculiar expression in it. He was gnawing his moustaches too. I am very fond of him, and I ran back to the chair and looked up and mewed, for I wanted to know what was the matter.

"You're a curious cat, Toots," said he; "but I suppose you're only like the rest of the world. I did think you did care a little bit for me. It's only the cream, is it, old fellow? As a companion, you prefer Terence? Eh? Well, off with you!"

But I need hardly say that I would not leave him. It was no want of love for him that led me to the saddle-room. I was not base enough to forget that he had been my friend in need, even if he had been less amiable to me since. All that evening I lay on his breast and slept. *But I dreamt of the mouse!*

The next morning he went out riding.

"He will not miss me now," thought I. "I will devote the morning to hunting through that wretched room inch by inch, for the last time. It will satisfy me that the mouse is not there, and it really is a duty to try and convince myself of this, that I may be cured of an infatuation which causes annoyance to so excellent a master."

I hurried off as rapidly as befitted the vigour of the

resolution, and when I got into the saddle-room I saw the mouse. And when the mouse saw me he fled like the wind.

I confess that I should have lost him then, but that a hole on which he had reckoned was stopped up, and he had to turn.

What a chase it was! Never did I meet his equal for audacity and fleetness. But I knew the holes as well as he did, and cut him off at every one. Round and round we went—behind the barrel, over the corn-chest, and then he made for the middle of the room.

Now, amongst all the rubbish which Terence had collected about him, there were many old articles of clothing belonging to the Captain, including a pair of long riding-boots, which had been gathering mildew, and stiffening out of shape in their present position ever since I came. One of these was lying on the floor; and just as I was all but upon the mouse, he darted into the boot.

A quiver of delight ran through me. With all his unwonted sagacity, Master Mouse had run straight into a trap. The boot was wide, and head and shoulders I plunged in after my prey.

I scented him all the way down the leg, but the painful fact is that I could not quite get to the bottom. He must have crouched in the toe or heel, and I could get no farther than the calf. Oh, if my master's legs had but been two inches shorter! I should have clawed into the remotest corner of the foot. As it was, I pushed, I struggled, I shook, I worried the wretched boot—but all in vain.

Only when I was all but choked did I withdraw my head for a gasp of fresh air. And there was the Captain himself, yelling with laughter, and sprawling all over the place in convulsions of unseemly merriment, with those long legs which—

but they are not his fault, poor man!

* * * * *

That is my story—an unfinished tale, of which I do not myself know the end. This is the one crook in my luxurious lot—that I cannot see the last of that mouse.

Happily, I don't think that my master any longer misunderstands my attachment to the saddle-room. The other day, he sat scribbling for a long time with a pencil and paper, and when he had done it, he threw the sketch to me and said, "There, Toots, look at that, and you will see what became of your friend!"

It was civilly meant, and I append the sketch for the sake of those whom it may inform. I do not understand pictures myself.

Those boots have a strange fascination for me now. I sit for hours by the mouth of the one where he went in and never came back. Not the faintest squeak from its recesses has ever stirred the sensitive hairs of my watchful ear. He must be starving, but not a nibble of the leather have I heard. I doze, but I am ever on the alert. Nightmares occasionally disturb me. I fancy I see him, made desperate by hunger, creep anxiously to the mouth of the boot, pricking his tagged ear. Once I had a terrible vision of his escaping, and of his tail as it vanished round the corner.

But these are dreams. He has never returned, I suspect that the truth is, that he had a fit from fright, in the toe of the boot, and is dead. Some day Terence will shake out his skeleton.

It grows very cold. This place is full of draughts, and the

Juliana Horatia Ewing

floor is damp.

He *must* be dead. He never could have lasted so long without a move or a nibble.

And it is tea-time. I think I shall join the Captain.

THE HENS OF HENCASTLE

(*Translated from the German of* VICTOR BLUeTHGEN)

What a hot, drowsy afternoon it was.

The blazing sun shone with such a glare upon the farmyard that it was almost unbearable, and there was not a vestige of grass or any green thing to relieve the eye or cast a little shade.

But the fowls in the back yard were not disturbed by the heat the least bit in the world, for they had plenty of time in which to doze, and they were fond of taking a siesta in the hottest place that could be found. Certainly the hottest place that afternoon, by far, was the yard in which they reposed.

There were five of them—a cock and four hens. Two of the hens were renowned throughout the whole village, for they wore tufts of feathers on their heads instead of the usual red combs; and the cock was very proud of having such distinguished-looking wives.

Besides which, he was naturally a very stately bird himself in appearance, and had a splendid blackish-green tail and a golden speckled hackle, which shone and glistened in the sun. He had also won many sharp battles with certain young cocks in the neighbourhood, whom curiosity about the tufted foreigners had attracted to the yard. The consequence of these triumphs was that he held undisputed dominion as far as the second fence from the farmyard, and whenever he shut his eyes and sounded his war-clarion, the whole of his rivals made off as fast as wings and legs could carry them.

So the five sat or stood by themselves in the yard, dozing in the sunshine, and they felt bored.

During the middle of the day they had managed to get some winks of sleep, but now the farmer's men began to thresh in a barn close by, making noise enough to wake the dead, so there was small chance of well-organized fowls being able to sleep through the din.

"I wish some one would tell a story," said one of the common hens, as she ruffled all her feathers up on end, and then shook them straight again, for coolness. "I am tired of scrabbling in the dust, and fly-catching is an amusement only suited to sparrows and such vulgar birds."

This was a hit at one of the foreign hens, who had wandered away a little and was pecking at flies on the wall. The two common hens were very fond of vexing the foreign ones, for their feelings were hurt at being reckoned less beautiful and rare.

The tufted fair one heard the remark, and called out spite-fully from a distance: "If certain people were not ignorant country bumpkins, they would be able to tell a good story themselves."

"That remark can't apply to me, for I know a great number of stories," replied the common hen, turning her head on one side to show her contempt. "For instance: once upon a time there was a hen who laid nothing but soft-shelled eggs—"

"You can't mean *me* by that story," said the tufted one, "for I have only laid one soft-shelled egg in my whole life. So there! But do tell me how your interesting story ends—I am so anxious to hear the end."

"You know that best yourself," retorted the other.

"Now I'm sure, dear Father Cock, you could tell us something really amusing if you would be so kind," said the second common hen, who was standing near him. "Those two make one's life a burthen, with their everlasting wrangling and bickering."

"Hush!" said the cock, who was standing motionless with one leg in the air, an attitude he often assumed when any very hard thinking had to be done; "I was just trying to recollect one."

After a pause, he said in a solemn voice: "I will tell you the terrible tale of the troubles of 'The Hens of Hencastle.'"

"Once upon a time—it was the village fair week, when, as you know, every one eats and drinks as much as he possibly can, and consequently a great many animals are killed,—the farmer's cook came into the fowlyard, and after carefully looking over all the chickens, remarked that seven of them would be twisting merrily on the spit next morning. On hearing this, all the fowls were plunged into the deepest despair, for no one felt sure that he would not be of the seven, and no one could guess how the victims would be chosen. Two young cockerels, in their deep perplexity, at last went to the yard-dog, Flaps by name, who was a very great friend of theirs, and to him they cackled out their woes.

Juliana Horatia Ewing

"'Why do you stop here?' asked Flaps. 'If you had any pluck at all you would run away.'"

"'Ah! Perhaps so—but who has enough courage for such a desperate step?' sighed the young cockerels. 'Why, you yourself are no more courageous than we, else why do you stop here chained up all day, and allow those tiresome children to come and tease you?'

"'Well,' replied the dog, 'I earn a good livelihood by putting up with these small discomforts, and besides that, *I* am not going to be set twisting on a spit. However, if you particularly wish it, we can go away somewhere together; but if we do, I may as well tell you at once, that you will have to feed me.'"

"The cockerels, fired by this bold advice, betook themselves at once to the henroost with the courage of young lions; and after a short but animated discussion, persuaded the whole of the cocks and hens to run away and to take Flaps as protector of the community."

"When darkness fell, the dog was unchained for the night as usual, and as soon as the coast seemed clear, he went to the henhouse, pushed back the sliding door with his nose, and let them all out."

"Then he and the whole company stole away as quietly as possible through the yard-gate, away out into the open country."

"The fowls flew and wandered on, the livelong night, perfectly happy in their freedom, and feeding themselves from the sheaves of corn that stood in the stubble-fields."

"Whenever Flaps felt hungry, the hens laid him a couple of

eggs or so which he found far nicer than barley-meal and dog-biscuit."

"When they passed through thinly-populated places where they were not likely to be observed, they marched gaily forward; but whenever there was a chance of danger, they only travelled by night."

"Meanwhile the cook went early in the morning to kill the chickens; but on finding the whole place as empty as Mother Hubbard's cupboard, she fell into a violent fit of hysterics, and the kitchen-maid and pig-boy had to put her under the pump, and work it hard for a quarter of an hour before they could revive her."

"After some days' journeying, the wanderers arrived at a large desolate-looking heath, in the middle of which stood an old weather-beaten house, apparently uninhabited. Flaps was sent forward to examine it, and he searched from garret to cellar without finding a trace of a human being. The fowls then examined the neighbourhood for two whole days and nights with a like result, and so they determined to take up their abode in the dwelling."

"In they trooped, and set themselves to work to turn it into a strong castle, well fortified against all danger. They stopped up the holes and cracks with tufts of grass, and piled a wall of big and little stones right round the house. When the repairs were completed they called it Hencastle."

"During the autumn some of the fowls ventured forth into the cornfields that lay near the haunts of men, and collected a store of grain to supply them with food during the winter. They kept it on the floor of a loft, and when spring came they sowed the remainder of the stock in a field, where it produced such an abundant crop that they had plenty of

Juliana Horatia Ewing

provisions for the following winter.

"Thus they lived a peaceful and happy life, which was so uneventful that it has no history; and Mark, the watchman, who always stood on the coping-stone of the highest chimney to act as sentinel, used constantly to fall asleep, partly from sheer boredom, and partly from the combined effects of old age, good living, and having nothing on earth to do. Flaps, too, who had undertaken to guard the castle against intruders, and who at first used to patrol the house carefully inside and out every night, soon came to the conclusion that the game was not worth the candle."

"One chilly evening, about the time of the first snows, when the wind was beginning to whistle over the heath and make strange noises in the castle, two old hens were up in the loft having a chat and picking up a few stray grains of corn for supper. All of a sudden they heard a mysterious 'Piep.' 'Hollo!' said one, 'what's that? no one can be hatching out at this time of the year—it's impossible; yet surely something said "Piep" down there in the corner.'"

"Just then another 'Piep' was heard."

"'I don't think it sounds *quite* like a young chicken,' replied the other hen."

"In the middle of their discussion on this knotty point, they descried a couple of mice at the edge of the corn-heap. One of them was sitting on his hind-legs, washing his ears and whiskers with his fore-paws, but his wife was gobbling up corn at a rapid rate, and in this sight the wise and far-seeing old hens discerned the probability of future troubles."

"'Hollo there! that's our corn,' they cried; 'you mustn't steal it. Of course you may have a few grains in the depth of winter to keep you from starving; but remember, when spring comes again, this sort of thing must stop, and you must go away and never come here any more.'"

"'Piep,' said the mice, and vanished."

"The two hens told the rest what had happened, but nobody troubled themselves about such an insignificant matter, and some said that the poor old things made mountains out of molehills. Anyhow, in two days everybody, including the wise hens themselves, had forgotten all about it. Later on, that winter, the mice had seven young ones—seven such skinny, thread-limbed, beady-eyed little beasts that no one noticed their arrival."

"Very soon after, almost before any hen had time to look round or think, behold! mice were squeaking in every corner, and there were holes behind every wainscot, plank, and rafter."

"A year passed away, and when winter returned again the mice came and took the stored corn away in such quantities that everybody saw none would be left to sow in the spring."

"Matters had come to a crisis; many and anxious discussions were held amongst the fowls, for good counsel was a thing much sought after at Hencastle."

"At first they took very energetic measures, and many a mouse fell a victim to a well-aimed peck from a cock's beak; but alas! the mice took energetic measures also, and resisted to the death, so that many a fowl's leg was bitten to the bone. Much had been said, and much was done, but the mice were more numerous than before."

"The commonwealth then decided on sending three

experienced cocks out into the world, to try and find some means for getting rid of the plague of mice."

"The cocks journeyed for one whole day without finding anything to help them in their trouble, but towards evening they came to a wild, rocky mountainside, full of caves and clefts, and made up their minds to stay there for the night; so they crept into a hole under a ledge of rock, put their heads under their wings, and went to sleep."

"In the middle of the night they were roused by the sound of flapping wings, followed by a whispering voice, saying, 'whish—ish,' which soon broke out into a loud 'Whoo—hoo! whoo—hoo!' They popped their heads out of the hole to see what was the matter, and they perceived a great owl sitting on a stump, flapping its wings up and down, and rolling its great round eyes about, which glared like red-hot coals in its head.

"'Mice here! Mice here! Whoo—hoo!' it shrieked.

"On hearing this the cocks nudged one another, and said, 'We are in luck's way at last.' Then as the owl still continued to call for mice, one of them plucked up courage and addressed it: 'If you will only come with us, sir, you shall have as many mice as you can eat—a whole house-full, if you like.'

"'Who may you be?' hissed the owl, and glared with its fiery eyes into the cleft."

"'We come from Hencastle, where there are hundreds of mice, who devour our corn day and night."

"'Whoo—hoo! I'll come, I'll come,' screamed the owl, snapping its beak with pleasure."

"In the grey of the dawn the fowls sat on the roof-tree, listening to Mark, the watchman, who stood on the top of, his chimney, and cried,

"What do I see?
Here come the three!
And with them, I reckon,
A bird with no neck on."

"Thereupon the owl and the three messengers flew up with a rush to the top of the castle."

"'Ha! ha! I smell mice,' shrieked the new comer, and dashed through a hole in the roof, from whence it shortly reappeared with a mouse in its claws."

"This sight filled all the fowls with joy; and as they sat on the edge of the roof in a row, they nudged each other, and remarked,

"This has indeed been a happy venture."

"For a few days everything went as smoothly as possible, but after a time the mice began to find out that the owl could only see really well at night, that it saw badly by day, and hardly at all when the midday sun was shining through the window into the loft. So they only came out at noon, and then dragged enough corn away into their holes to last them till the following day.

"One night the owl did not catch a single mouse, and so, being very hungry, drove its beak into some hen's eggs that lay in a corner, and ate them. Finding them more to its taste than the fattest mouse, and much less trouble to catch, henceforth the owl gave up mouse-hunting, and took to egg-poaching. This the fowls presently discovered, and the three

Juliana Horatia Ewing

wise cocks were sent to tell the owl to go away, as it was no longer of use to anybody, for it never caught mice but only ate eggs.

"'Whoo—hoo! whoo—hoo! More eggs—give me more eggs, or I'll scratch your eyes out,' shrieked the owl, and began to whet its beak on a beam in such a savage manner that the three cocks fled in terror to the top of the chimney."

"Having somewhat recovered from their alarm, they went down and told Flaps, who was basking in the sunshine, that the owl must be got rid of."

"'What, are all the mice eaten, then?' inquired he."

"'Alas!' answered one of the cocks, 'the brute will eat nothing but eggs now, and threatens to scratch our eyes out if we don't supply as many more as it wants.'"

"'Wait till noonday,' said the dog, 'and I'll soon bring the rascal to reason.'"

"At twelve o'clock Flaps quietly pushed the door open and went up into the loft. There sat the old owl winking and blinking in a corner."

"'So you are the robber who is going to scratch people's eyes out,' said Flaps. 'For this you must die!'"

"'That remains to be seen,' sneered the owl; 'but eyes I will have, and dogs' eyes too!' and with that it swooped down upon Flaps' head; but the old dog seized the bird between his teeth and killed it, though not before one of his own eyes had been scratched out in the struggle."

"'No matter,' said Flaps; 'I've done my duty, at any rate, and I don't know why I should want more than one eye to see with;' and so saying, he went back to his post."

"The fowls made a great feast, which lasted the whole day, to celebrate the owl's death."

"But the mice remained in the castle, and continued to increase and multiply. So the three wise cocks had to go forth on a second voyage of discovery, in order to try and find a remedy against the intruders."

"They flew on for a night and a day without any result; but towards morning, on the second day, they alighted to rest in a thick wood, and there, in one of the forest glades, just as the sun was rising, they saw a red-coated animal watching a mouse-hole. It was a fox, who had come out to find something for breakfast. They soon saw him catch a mouse and eat it, and then heard him say, 'Heaven be praised for small mercies! I have managed to secure a light breakfast at last, though I've been hunting all night in vain.'

"'Do you hear that?' said one of the messengers. 'He considers himself very lucky to have caught a single mouse. That's the sort of animal we want.'"

"So the cock called down from the tree—'I say! below there! Mr. Mouse-eater! you can have a whole loft-full of such long-tailed vermin as that, if you will come with us. But you must first solemnly swear that you will never eat eggs instead of mice.'"

"'Nothing on earth shall ever tempt me to touch an egg. I swear it most solemnly,' said the fox, staring up into the tree. 'But whence do you come, my worthy masters?'"

"'We live at Hencastle, but no one knows where that is

　　　　Juliana Horatia Ewing

except the mice, who eat us out of house and home.'"

"'You don't say so,' said the fox from below, licking his lips. 'And are there many more such handsome, magnificent birds as you are, at Hencastle?'"

"Why, of course, the whole place is full of them."

"'Then I'll come with you,' said the fox, lowering his eyes, lest the cocks should discern the hungry look in them. 'And if there are a thousand mice in the loft, they shall all soon lick the dust. Ah! you don't know what delicious dainties such—mice—are.'"

"This time the fowls had to wait till evening before they heard Mark, the watchman, crowing from his chimney, and calling forth,

"Here come the three!
But what do I see?
Why, the friend that they bring
Is a four-legged thing."

"When the fox got to the outer wall, he sniffed about uneasily and said,

"I smell a dog, and I am not fond of the race, nor do they as a rule like me."

"'You need not be alarmed,' replied the cocks; 'there is only one of them here—our friend Mr. Flaps,—and he is always stationed outside the castle; besides, he is just as glad as we are that you have come to kill the mice.'"

"But in spite of this assurance, the fox did not at all like the idea of going in past Flaps, who stood at the door, showing his teeth, and with the hair down his back standing on end; but at last, catching sight of a number of plump young chickens looking out at a window, Reynard could resist no longer, and with his mouth watering in anxiety to be among them, he slipped past Flaps like lightning, and scampered up into the loft. Once there, he behaved so affably to the fowls, and especially to some of the oldest and most influential hens, that very soon every one looked on him as their friend in time of need, and their enthusiasm was brought to a climax when they saw him catch four mice in half as many minutes.

"In the dead of the night, when all were asleep, Reynard crept up to where the fowls roosted, and finding out where the youngest and fattest were perched, he snapped off the heads of a couple before they had even time to flutter a feather. He then carried them to the window, opened it very gently, dropped the dead bodies out on to the ground beneath, and then sped away down to the house-door and bolted it."

"When he had done this, he returned to the old hens and woke them by groaning in such a heartbreaking manner, that all the fowls crowded round him to know what was amiss."

"'Alas!' cried he, 'it has been my sad lot to witness a most fearful sight. That dog whom you keep down below to guard the house slipped in at the door, and going to the corner where the lovely young chickens roost, quicker than thought killed two that were more beautiful than angels. I was chasing a mouse under the stairs at the time, and happened to come up just as the dreadful deed was done, and I saw the robber making off with his booty. Only come with me a minute, and you shall see that I have spoken the truth.'"

"He took the scared and frightened fowls to the window, and

when they looked out, they saw to their horror their guardian Flaps sniffing at the dead bodies on the ground outside. "

"'Who would have thought it!' said the hens, in an awe-stricken whisper."

"'You may thank me,' said the fox, 'for my presence of mind in bolting the house-door when he ran out, or no one knows how many more he would have killed! If you will take my advice, you will send him about his business; and if you will put me in his place, I can assure you that you shall be protected in quite another manner.'"

"'Hi! open the door,' cried Flaps, who saw something was wrong; 'you've got another King Stork, I'll be bound.' But though he rattled and shook the door, no one unbolted it. 'Ah!' sighed Flaps, 'before long the whole pack of idiots will be killed and eaten.' So he scratched open an old hole in the wall that had been stopped up, and crept in. He arrived just in time to hear the old hens giving orders that no more eggs were to be given him, and that the door was to be kept bolted, in order that he might be obliged either to leave the place or to starve."

"They were all talking at once, and so eagerly, that no one noticed the dog come up behind them. He gave one spring and seized the fox by the throat. The attack was quite unexpected, but the fox fought, writhed, and wriggled like an eel, and just as he was being borne down, he made one desperate snap, and bit off the dog's ear close to the head."

"'Well, my ear is done for, but so is this blood-thirsty villain,' said Flaps, looking down at the fox, which lay dead at his feet; 'and as for you, you pack of ungrateful fools, one ear is quite enough to listen to you with. Here have I been your faithful comrade for all these years, and yet you believe that

I have turned murderer in my old age on the word of this rogue, who did the evil deed himself last night.'"

"Now that the panic was over, the fowls felt heartily ashamed of themselves for having been deceived by the fox, and done Flaps such great injustice. So they all asked his pardon, and the feast which they held to celebrate their deliverance from the fox was even more magnificent than the last, and it went on for two whole days.

"Hencastle was *en fete* for a time, but it was a very short time. For the mice were no less glad than the fowls that their enemy was dead; and now that both he and the owl had disappeared, they came out fearlessly at all hours of the day, and lived a life quite free from trouble and care."

"Not so the fowls. What was to be done with the ever-increasing colony of corn-stealers? The more the fowls meditated, the more the mice squeaked and played about, and the more corn they dragged away into their holes. There was even a rumour that some one meddled with the eggs."

"There was nothing for it but to dispatch the three messengers a third time, with directions to be more vigilant and careful than before. Away they flew, farther than ever. The first chance of help that arose was from a couple of cats and a kite, who seemed likely to perform the required work, but the cocks declined to accept their aid, feeling that the Hencastle had suffered too much already from two-winged and four-legged protectors."

"At length the messengers reached a bit of waste ground close to a village, and there they saw an extremely grimy-looking gipsy sitting on a bank. He knocked the ashes out of his black pipe, and muttered, 'I've the luck of a dog! Here am I with a lot of the best mouse-traps in the world, and I

Juliana Horatia Ewing

haven't sold one this blessed day!'"

"'Here's luck!' said the wise birds. 'That is exactly the man for us; he is neither two-winged nor four-legged, so he will be quite safe.'"

"They flew down at once to the rat-catcher and made their proposition. He laughed softly and pleasantly to himself, and accepted their invitation without any demur, and started at once with a light step and lighter heart for Hencastle."

"Two days after this, the fowls heard Mark, the watchman, crowing away lustily from his chimney-pot,

"What do I see?
Here come the three!
And the black beast they bring
Has no tail and no wing."

"'But,' added the sentinel in less official language, 'he carries a bundle of things that look like little houses made of wire.'"

"The gipsy was at once taken up to the loft, and having, luckily, a few scraps of strong-smelling bacon left over from his last night's supper, he struck a light and managed to make a small fire in the long-disused grate with some bits of dry grass and chips. He then frizzled some bacon and baited his traps, and in less than ten minutes he had filled them all, for the mice had never smelt such a delicious thing as fried bacon before, and besides, they were new to the wiles of man."

"The fowls were wild with delight, and in their thankfulness they bethought them of a special mark of favour, and every hen came clucking up to him and laid an egg at his feet."

"For about a week the gipsy did nothing but catch mice and eat eggs; but all things must have an end, and the bacon ran out, just when the gipsy had come to the conclusion that he was heartily sick of egg-diet. Being a man of action, he put out his hand suddenly and caught the fattest and nicest young chicken within reach, and promptly wrung its neck."

"Oh, what a row there was in the henroost! The cocks began to crow loud enough to split their throats, and the hens to fly about and cackle. The man was nearly deafened, and yelled out at the top of his voice, 'What do you expect, you fools? Mice can only be caught with meat, and meat I must and will have too.' He then let them rave on, and quietly and methodically continued to pluck his chicken. When it was ready, he made a fire and began to roast it."

"In the meanwhile, Flaps had heard all the noise and outcry, and as it showed no signs of abating, he thought the man was most likely in mischief, so he went into the castle."

"'Oh! Woe! Misery! Horror! Despair!' cried all the fowls at once as soon as they saw him. 'The murderer has slain young Scratchfoot the cock, and is just going to roast him!'"

"'You're a dead man,' growled Flaps to the rat-catcher, as soon as he got up to the loft."

"'I'm not so sure of that, my fine cur,' said the man, taking hold of the cudgel he had brought with him, and tucking up his sleeves."

"But the brave old dog sprang at him and bit him so severely that he uttered a savage groan, and dealt Flaps a heavy blow with his cudgel. This nearly broke the dog's leg and obliged him to relax his hold, on which the gipsy dashed down-stairs and ran away with such speed that Flaps on three legs had no

Juliana Horatia Ewing

chance of overtaking him."

"'Wait a bit!' cried the man from afar. 'I'll remember you!' And then his retreating figure became smaller and smaller on the heath until at last it disappeared altogether."

"This time the fowls had no heart for a feast. They sat brooding and moping in rows on the rafters, for they began to see very clearly that it was quite hopeless to try and get rid of the mice."

"Poor old Flaps, too, was very ill. A good many days elapsed before he could get about, and for years he walked lame on his injured leg."

"One morning as the fowls were listlessly wandering about, wondering what was to happen next, Mark, the watchman, was heard crowing away in a very excited manner,

"What do I see?
Twenty and three!"

"'What do you see?' cried they all in a great fright. 'Twenty and three what?'"

"'An army of soldiers dressed in smock frocks. They are armed with pitchforks, and the black gipsy is their general.'"

"The fowls flew up like a cloud to the roof, and sure enough they saw the rat-catcher coming across the heath with a crowd of villagers towards the castle."

"When they broke the doleful news to Flaps, he said, 'That scoundrel of a man has betrayed our hiding-place, and we must wander forth again. Get ready, and keep up your spirits, and remember that in any case we should not have been able to stay here much longer, on account of the mice.'

"So the hens filled their crops as full as possible, and escaped with Flaps out at the back door."

"When the country-folk got to the house, they found nothing in it but a small heap of corn; so they fell upon the gipsy and half killed him for having brought them on a fool's errand. Then they divided what little corn there was left, and went away."

"As to the mice they were left to whistle for their food."

"So ends the tale of the Hens of Hencastle."

"And a very fine tale too," said one of the stranger-hens who had been asleep all the time, and woke up with a jump. "It was deeply interesting." The threshers happened to have stopped to rest for a moment, or she would never have woke at all.

"Of course it was!" said the cock, full of dignity; and he shook his feathers straight.

"But what became of the fowls afterwards?" asked one of the common hens.

"I never tell a hen a secret," said the cock; and he strutted off to hunt for worms.

FLAPS

A SEQUEL TO "THE HENS OF HENCASTLE"

And what became of Flaps after they all left Hencastle? Well, he led his company on and on, but they could find no suitable place to settle in; and when the fowls recovered from their fright, they began to think that they had abandoned the castle too hastily, and to lay the blame on Flaps.

Mark himself said that he might have overestimated the number of the invaders. There might not have been twenty-three, but really Flaps was in such a hurry for the news, and one must say something when it was one's duty to make a report.

The three wise cocks objected to speak of themselves or their services, but they had had some experience on behalf of the community in times of danger, and in their opinion there had been a panic, and the hasty action taken by Flaps was injudicious and regrettable.

The oldest hen of Hencastle shook her feathers to show how much Flaps was in the wrong, and then puffed them out to show how much she was in the right; and after clearing her throat almost as if she were going to crow, she observed very shrilly that she "didn't care who contradicted her when she said that the common sense of the Mother of a Family was enough to tell *her* that an old dog, who had lost an eye and an ear and a leg, was no fit protector for the feminine and the young and the inexperienced."

The chief cock was not so free of his opinions as the chief hen, but he grumbled and scolded about everything, by which one may make matters amply unpleasant without committing oneself or incurring responsibility.

Another of the hens made a point of having no opinion. She said that was her way, she trusted everybody alike and bore her share of suffering, which was seldom small, without a murmur. But her good wishes were always at any one's service, and she would say that she sincerely hoped that a sad injustice had not been done to the red-haired gentleman with the singularly agreeable manners, who would have been gatekeeper of Hencastle at this moment if it had not been for Flaps.

Poor Flaps! Well might he say, "One ear is enough to listen to you with, you pack of ungrateful fools!"

He was beginning to find out that, as a rule, the Helpless have a nice way with them of flinging all their cares upon the Helpful, and reserving their own energies to pick holes in what is done on their behalf; and that they are apt to flourish, in good health and poor spirits, long after such friends as Flaps have been worn out, bit by bit, in their service.

"First an eye, then an ear, then a leg," the old dog growled to himself; "and there's not a fowl with a feather out of him. But I've done my duty, and that's enough."

Matters went from bad to worse. The hens had no corn, and

Juliana Horatia Ewing

Flaps got no eggs, and the prospect of either home or food seemed very remote. One evening it was very rainy, the fowls roosted in a walnut-tree for shelter, and Flaps fell asleep at the foot of it.

"Could anything be more aggravating than that creature's indifference?" said Hen No. 2. "Here we sit, wet to the skin, and there he lies asleep! Dear me! I remember one of my neck feathers got awry once, at dear old Hencastle (the pencilling has been a good deal admired in my time, though I say it that shouldn't), and the Red-haired Gentleman noticed it in a moment. I remember he put his face as close to mine as I am to you, but in the most gentlemanly manner, and murmured so softly,

"'Excuse me—there's just one of those lovely little feathers the least bit in the world—'"

"I believe it was actually between his lips, when we were interrupted, and I had to put it tidy myself. But we might all be plucked as bare as poor young Scratchfoot before Flaps would think of smoothing us down. Just hear how he snores! Ah! it's a trying world, but I never complain."

"I do, though," said the chief hen. "I'm not one to put up with neglect. Hi, there! are you asleep?" And scratching a bit of the rough bark off the walnut-tree, she let it drop on to Flaps' nose.

"I'm awake," said Flaps; "what's the matter?"

"I never knew any one snore when he was awake before," said the hen; and all the young cockerels chuckled.

"Well, I believe I was napping," said Flaps. "Damp weather always makes me sleepy, and I was dreaming of the old farmyard."

"Poor old farm!" sighed Hen No. 2. "We had board and lodging there, at any rate."

"And now we've neither," said Hen No. 1. "Mr. Flaps, do you know that we're wet to the skin, and dying of starvation, whilst you put your nose into your great-coat pocket and go to sleep?"

"You're right," said Flaps. "Something must be done this evening. But I see no use in taking the whole community about in the rain. We will send out another expedition."

"Cock-a-doodle-doo!" screamed the three wise ones; "that means that we're to face the storm whilst you have another nap, eh?"

"It seems an odd thing," said the chief cock, scratching his comb with his claw, "that Flaps never thinks of going himself on these expeditions."

"You're right," said Flaps. "It is an odd thing, for times out of mind I've heard our old friend, the farmer, say, 'If you want a thing done—Go; if not—Send.' This time I shall go. Cuddle close to each other, and keep up your spirits. I'll find us a good home yet."

The fowls were much affected by Flaps' magnanimity, and with one voice they cried: "Thank you, dear Flaps. Whatever you decide upon will do for us."

And Mark added, "I will continue to act as watchman." And he went up to the top of the tree as Flaps trotted off down the muddy road.

Juliana Horatia Ewing

All that evening and far into the night it rained and rained, and the fowls cuddled close to each other to keep warm, and Flaps did not return. In the small hours of the morning the rain ceased, and the rain-clouds drifted away, and the night-sky faded and faded till it was dawn.

"Cock-a-doodle-doo!" said Mark, and all the fowls woke up.

"What do you see and hear from the tree-top, dear Mark?" said they. "Is Flaps coming?"

> "Not a thing can I see
> From the top of the tree,
> But a long, winding lane
> That is sloppy with rain;"

replied Mark. And the fowls huddled together again, and put their heads back under their wings.

Paler and paler grew the grey sky, and at last it was broken with golden bars, and at the first red streak that caught fire behind them, Mark crowed louder than before, and all the hens of Hencastle roused up for good.

"What do you see and hear from the tree-top, dear Mark?" they inquired. "Is Flaps coming?"

> "Not a sound do I hear,
> And I very much fear
> That Flaps, out of spite,
> Has deserted us quite;"

replied Mark. And the fowls said nothing, for they were by no means at ease in their consciences.

Their delight was proportionably great when, a few minutes later, the sentinel sang out from his post,

"Here comes Flaps, like the mail!
And he's waving his tail."

"Well, dear, dear Flaps!" they all cackled as he came trotting up, "where is our new home, and what is it like?"

"Will there be plenty to eat?" asked the cocks with one crow.

"Plenty," replied Flaps.

"Shall we be safe from mice, owls, wild beasts, and wild men?" cried the hens.

"You will," answered Flaps.

"Is it far, dear Flaps?"

"It is very near," said Flaps; "but I may as well tell you the truth at once—it's a farmyard."

"Oh!—" said all the fowls.

"We may be roasted, or have our heads chopped off," whimpered the young cockerels.

"Well, Scratchfoot was roasted at Hencastle," said Flaps; "and he wasn't our only loss. One can't have everything in this world; and I assure you, if you could see the poultry-yard—so dry under foot, nicely wired in from marauders; the most charming nests, with fresh hay in them; drinking-troughs; and then at regular intervals, such abundance of corn, mashed potatoes, and bones, that my own mouth watered at—are served out—"

"That sounds good," said the young cockerels.

"Ahem! ahem!" said the chief cock. "Did you see anything very remarkable—were the specimens of my race much superior in strength and good looks?—"

"My dear cock!" said Flaps; "there's not a tail or a comb or a hackle to touch you. You'll be cock of the walk in no time."

"Ahem! ahem!" said the chief cock modestly. "I have always had a sort of fatality that way. Pray, my dears, don't look so foolish and deplorable, but get the young people together, and let us make a start. Mr. Flaps is a person of strong common sense, a quality for which I myself have always been remarkable, and I thoroughly endorse and support his excellent advice, of which I am the best judge. I have very much regretted of late to observe a tendency in this family (I say a tendency, for I hope it goes no further) to undervalue Mr. Flaps, and even (I hardly like to allude to such reprehensible and disgusting absurdity) to recall the memory of a vulgar red-haired impostor, who gained a brief entrance into our family circle. I am not consulted as I should be in these fluctuations of opinion, but there are occasions when it is necessary that the head of a family should exercise his discretion and his authority, and, so to speak, put down his claw. I put down my claw. We are going to Mr. Flaps' farmyard. Cock-a-doodle-doo Cock-a-doodle-doo!"

Now, when the head of a family says "Cock-a-doodle-doo!" there is nothing more to be said. So to the farmyard the whole lot of them went, and were there before the sun got one golden hair of his head over the roof of the big barn.

And only Mark, as they all crowded into their new home, turned his head round over his back to say: "And you, Flaps; what shall you do?"

"Oh, I shall be all right," said Flaps. "Good-bye and good luck to you."

It cannot be said that Flaps was positively in high spirits when he had settled his proteges in their new home in the farmyard, and was left alone; but there are some good folk who contrive to make duty do the work of pleasure in this life, and then a piece of business fairly finished is as good as a treat.

It is not bread and bones, however, and Flaps was very hungry—so hungry that he could not resist the temptation to make his way towards the farmhouse, on the chance of picking up some scraps outside. And that was how it came about, that when the farmer's little daughter Daisy, with a face like the rosy side of a white-heart cherry set deep in a lilac print hood, came back from going with the dairy lass to fetch up the cows, she found Flaps snuffing at the back door, and she put her arms round his neck (they reached right round with a little squeezing) and said:

"Oh, I never knew you'd be here so early! You nice thing!"

And Flaps' nose went right into the print hood, and he put out his tongue and licked Daisy's face from the point of her chin up her right cheek to her forehead, and then from her forehead down her left cheek back to her chin, and he found that she was a very nice thing too.

But the dairymaid screamed, "Good gracious! where did that nasty strange dog come from? Leave him alone, Miss Daisy, or he'll bite your nose off."

"He won't!" said Daisy indignantly. "He's the dog Daddy promised me;" and the farmer coming out at that minute, she ran up to him crying, "Daddy! Isn't this my dog?"

Juliana Horatia Ewing

"Bless the child, no!" said the farmer; "it's a nice little pup I'm going to give thee. Where did that dirty old brute come from?"

"He would wash," said little Daisy, holding very fast to Flaps' coat.

"Fine washing too!" said the dairymaid, "And his hair's all lugs."

"I could comb them," said Daisy.

"He's no but got one eye," said the swineherd. "Haw! haw! haw!"

"He sees me with the other," said Daisy. "He's looking up at me now."

"And one of his ears gone!" cried the dairy lass. "He! he! he!"

"Perhaps I could make him a cap," said Daisy, "as I did when my doll lost her wig. It had pink ribbons and looked very nice."

"Why, he's lame of a leg," guffawed the two farming-men. "See, missy, he hirples on three."

"I can't run very fast," said Daisy, "and when I'm old enough to, perhaps his leg will be well."

"Why, you don't want this old thing for a play-fellow, child?" said the farmer.

"I do! I do!" wept Daisy.

"But why, in the name of whims and whamsies?"

"Because I love him," said Daisy.

When it comes to this with the heart, argument is wasted on the head; but the farmer-went on: "Why he's neither useful nor ornamental. He's been a good dog in his day, I dare say; but now—"

At this moment Flaps threw his head up in the air and sniffed, and his one eye glared, and he set his teeth and growled.

He smelt the gipsy, and the gipsy's black pipe, and every hair stood on end with rage.

"The dog's mad!" cried the swineherd, seizing a pitchfork.

"You're a fool," said the farmer (who wasn't). "There's some one behind that haystack, and the old watch-dog's back is up. See! there he runs; and as I'm a sinner, it's that black rascal who was loitering round, the day my ricks were fired, and you lads let him slip. Off after him, for I fancy I see smoke." And the farmer flew to his haystacks.

Hungry and tired as he was, Flaps would have pursued his old enemy, but Daisy would not let him go. She took him by the ear and led him indoors to breakfast instead. She had a large basin of bread-and-milk, and she divided this into two portions, and gave one to Flaps and kept the other for herself. And as she says she loves Flaps, I leave you to guess who got most bread-and-milk.

That was how the gipsy came to live for a time in the county gaol, where he made mouse-traps rather nicely for the good of the rate-payers.

Juliana Horatia Ewing

And that was how Flaps, who had cared so well for others, was well cared for himself, and lived happily to the end of his days.

*   *   *   *   *

"Why, it's in print!" said Father Cock; "and I said as plain as any cock could crow, that it was a secret. Now, who let it out?"

"Don't talk to me about secrets," said the fair foreigner; "I never trouble my head about such things."

"Some people are very fond of drawing attention to their heads," said the common hen; "and if other people didn't think more of a great unnatural-looking chignon than of all the domestic virtues put together, they might have their confidences respected."

"I's all very well," said Father Cock, "but you're all alike. There's not a hen can know a secret without going and telling it."

"Well, come!" said a little Bantam hen, who had newly arrived; "whichever hen told it, the cock must have told it first."

"What's that ridiculous nonsense your talking?" cried the cock; and he ran at her and pecked her well with his beak.

"Oh! oh! oh!" cried the Bantam.

Dab, dab, dab, pecked the cock.

"Now! has anybody else got anything to say on the subject?"

But nobody had. So he flew up on to the wall, and cried "Cock-a-doodle-doo!"

Juliana Horatia Ewing

A WEEK SPENT IN A GLASS POND

BY THE GREAT WATER-BEETLE

Very few beetles have ever seen a Glass Pond. I once spent a week in one, and though I think, with good management, and in society suitably selected, it may be a comfortable home enough, I advise my water-neighbours to be content with the pond in the wood.

The story of my brief sojourn in the Glass Pond is a story with a moral, and it concerns two large classes of my fellow-creatures: those who live in ponds and—those who don't. If I do not tell it, no one else will. Those connected with it who belong to the second class (namely, Francis, Molly, and the learned Doctor, their grandfather) will not, I am sure. And as to the rest of us, there is none left but—

However, that is the end of my tale, not the beginning.

The beginning, as far as I am concerned, was in the Pond. It is very difficult to describe a pond to people who cannot live under water, just as I found it next door to impossible to make a minnow I knew believe in dry land. He said, at last, that perhaps there might be some little space beyond the pond in hot weather, when the water was low; and that was the utmost that he would allow. But of all cold-blooded unconvinceable creatures, the most obstinate are fish.

Men are very different. They do not refuse to believe what lies beyond their personal experience. I respected the learned Doctor, and was really sorry for the disadvantages under which he laboured. That a creature of his intelligence should have only two eyes, and those not even compound ones— that he should not be able to see under water or in the dark— that he should not only have nothing like six legs, but be quite without wings, so that he could not even fly out of his own window for a turn in the air on a summer's evening— these drawbacks made me quite sorry for him; for he had none of the minnow's complacent ignorance. He knew my advantages as well as I knew them myself, and bore me no ill-will for them.

"The *Dyticus marginalis*, or Great Water-Beetle," I have heard him say, in the handsomest manner, "is equally at home in the air, or in the water. Like all insects in the perfect state, it has six legs, of which the hindmost pair are of great strength, and fringed so as to serve as paddles. It has very powerful wings, and, with Shakespeare's witches, it flies by night. It has two simple, and two sets of compound eyes. When it goes below water, it carries a stock of air with it, on the diving-bell principle; and when this is exhausted, comes to the surface, tail uppermost, for a fresh supply. It is the most voracious of the carnivorous water-beetles."

The last sentence is rather an unkind reflection on my good appetite, but otherwise the Doctor spoke handsomely of me, and without envy.

And yet I am sure it could have been no matter of wonder if my compound eyes, for instance, had been a very sore subject with a man who knew of them, and whose one simple pair were so nearly worn out.

More than once, when I have seen the old gentleman put a green shade on to his reading-lamp, and glasses before his eyes, I have felt inclined to hum,—"Ah, my dear Doctor, if you could only take a cool turn in the pond! You would want no glasses or green shades, where the light comes tenderly subdued through water and water-weeds."

Indeed, after living, as I can, in all three—water, dry land, and air,—I certainly prefer to be under water. Any one whose appetite is as keen, and whose hind-legs are as powerful as mine, will understand the delights of hunting, and being hunted, in a pond; where the light comes down in fitful rays and reflections through the water, and gleams among the hanging roots of the frog-bit, and the fading leaves of the water-starwort, through the maze of which, in and out, hither and thither, you pursue, and are pursued, in cool and skilful chase, by a mixed company of your neighbours, who dart, and shoot, and dive, and come and go, and any one of whom at any moment may either eat you or be eaten by you.

And if you want peace and quiet, where can one bury oneself so safely and completely as in the mud? A state of existence, without mud at the bottom, must be a life without repose.

I was in the mud one day, head downwards, when human voices came to me through the water. It was summer, and the pond was low at the time.

"Oh, Francis! Francis! The Water-Soldier[D] is in flower."

"Hooray! Dig him up for the aquarium! Grandfather says it's very rare—doesn't he?"

"He says it's not at all common; and there's only one, Francis. It would be a pity if we didn't get it up by the roots, and it died."

"Nonsense, Molly. I'll get it up. But let's get the beasts first. You get the pickle-jar ready, whilst I fix the stick on to the colander."

"Does cook know you've taken it, Francis?"

"By this time she does, I should think. Look here, Molly—I wish you would try and get this stick right. It wants driving through the handles. I'm just going to have a look at the Water-Soldier."

"You always give me the work to do," Molly complained; and as she spoke, I climbed up an old stake that was firmly planted in the mud, and seated myself on the top, which stood out of the water, and looked at her.

She was a neat-looking little soul, with rosy cheeks, and a resolute expression of countenance. She looked redder and firmer than usual as she drove the broomstick through the handles of the colander, whilst the boy was at the other side of the pond with the Water-Soldier, whose maiden-blossom shone white among its sword-leaves.

It shone in the sunshine which came gaily through a gap in the trees, and warmed my coat through to my wings, and made the pond look lovely. That greedy *Ranatra*, who eats so much, and never looks a bit the more solid for his meals, crept up a reed and sunned his wings; the water-gnats skimmed and skated about, measuring the surface of the water with their long legs; the "boatmen" shot up and down till one was quite giddy, showing the white on their bodies, like swallows wheeling for their autumn-flight. Even the water-scorpion moved slowly over a sunny place from the roots of an arrow-head lily to a dark corner under the duck-weed.

Juliana Horatia Ewing

"Molly!" shouted the boy; "I wish you'd come and give a pull at the Water-Soldier. I've nearly got him up; but the leaves cut my hands, and you've got gloves. If the colander is ready, I'll begin to fish. There's a beetle on that stick. I wish I were near enough, I could snatch him up like anything."

"I wouldn't advise you to," said Molly. "Grandfather says that water-beetles have got daggers in their tails. Besides, some of the beetles are very greedy and eat the fish."

"The Big Black one doesn't," said Francis. "He said so. *Hydroeus piceus* is the name, and I dare say that's the one. It's the biggest of all the water-beetles and very harmless."

"He *may* be a good one," said Molly, looking thoughtfully and unmistakably at me, "but then he may be one of the bad ones; and if he is, he'll eat everything before him."

But by this time Francis was dipping the colander in and out on the opposite side, and she was left to struggle with the Water-Soldier.

"He's up at last," she announced, and the Soldier was landed on the bank.

"Come round," said the boy; "I've filled three jars."

"I hope you've been careful, Francis. You know Grandfather says that to stock a fresh-water aquarium is like the puzzle of the Fox and the Geese and the bag of seed. It's no use our having things that eat each other."

"They must eat something," said the boy; "they're used to it at home; and I wish you wouldn't be always cramming Grandfather down my throat. I want to do my aquarium my own way; and I gave most towards buying the bell-glass, so it's more mine than yours."

"Well, do as you like; only let us have plenty of water-boatmen," said Molly.

"I've got half-a-dozen at least; and the last sweep I went very low, quite in the mud, and I've got some most horrid things. There's one of them like a flat-iron, with pincers at the point."

"That's a water-scorpion. Oh, Francis! he eats dreadfully."

"I don't believe he can, he's so flat. Molly, is that nasty-looking thing a dragon-fly larva?"

"I believe it is; for there is the mask. You know his face is so ugly nothing would come near him if he didn't wear a mask. Then he lifts it up and snaps suddenly; *he* really *does* eat everything!"

"Well, I can't help it. I must have him. I want to see him hatch; and I shall plant a bullrush for him to climb up."

"I found a caddis-worm, with a beautifully built house, in the roots of the Water-Soldier, and I'm going to look along the edge for some shells. We must have shell-fish, you know, to keep the aquarium clean. Oh!"

"What is it, Molly? What have you found?"

"Oh, such a lovely spider! A water-spider—a scarlet spider. He's very small, but such a colour! Francis dear, may I keep him all to myself? I don't think I *can* let him go in with the others. If the dragon-fly larva ate him, I should never forgive myself, and you know you don't know for certain that the beetle is *Hydroeus piceus*. I shall give him an aquarium of

Juliana Horatia Ewing

his very own in a green finger-glass, with nothing but a little very nice duckweed, and one small snail to keep it clean, like a general servant. May I, Francis?"

"By all means. I don't want your scarlet spider. I can get lots more." He went on dipping with the colander, and she began to dig up water-plants and lay them in a heap. I sat and watched them, but the *Ranatra* got nervous and tried to go below. As usual, the dry bristles in his tail would not pierce the water without a struggle, and after floundering in the most ludicrous fashion for a few minutes, he fell straight into the colander, and was put into one of the pickle-jars.

"I've got enough now," said the boy, "and I want to go home and see about my net. I must have some fish. Can you carry the plants, Molly?"

"I'll manage," said Molly. "Now I'm ready."

"Wait a minute, though—I'd forgotten the beetle."

When I heard this I dropped into the water; but somehow or other I turned over very clumsily, and, like the *Ranatra*, I fell through into the colander, and was transferred to a pickle-jar.

Anything more disagreeable than being shaken up in a glass bottle, with beetles, and boatmen, and larvae of all sorts and sizes, including a dragon-fly in the second stage of his career, I can hardly imagine. When they took us out and put us into the glass pond, matters were certainly better, though there is a vast difference between a glass pond and a pond in a wood.

The first day it was by no means a bad imitation of a real pond, except for the want of a bed of mud. Molly had covered the bottom of the glass with gravel which she had steadily washed till water would run clear from it, in spite of the impatient exclamations of Francis, that it "would do now," and quite regardless of the inconvenience to which I was subjected by being kept in the pickle-jar. In this gravel she had embedded the roots of some Water Crowfoot and other pond-plants. The stones in the middle were nicely arranged, and well covered with moss and water-weeds. When water had been poured in up to the brim of the bell-glass, and we had been emptied out of the jars, the dragon-fly larva got into a good hole among the stones and ate most of the May-fly grubs, water-shrimps, and so forth, as they came into sight. I did not do badly myself, and only the bigger and stronger members of our society and a few skins were there next day, when Francis brought a jar full of minnows, a small carp, and a bull's-head, and turned them out in our midst.

"How they dart and swim round and round!" he exclaimed.

"Splendid," said Molly. "I *am* so sorry I am going away just now. You will try and keep the water fresh, won't you?"

"Of course I will. And let me have the scarlet spider whilst you are away. I couldn't find another."

"Well, if you must; but do take care, Francis. And here are the two bits of gutta-percha tubing to make into syphons. You must put them into hot water for a minute before you bend them, you know."

"I'll do it to-morrow, Molly; I have nothing else *to* do, you know, because Edward Brown won't be back for three or four days. So we can do nothing about the cricket club."

It was on the third day, when both the pieces of gutta-percha tubing were in a wash-hand basin of hot water, and the dragon-fly larva and I were finishing a minnow, with the help of the water-scorpion, that Master Edward Brown arrived unexpectedly, and so pressed his friend Francis to come out and consult "just for two minutes," and so delayed him when he got him, that the tubing melted into a shapeless lump, and the carp died unnoticed by any one but myself.

On the fourth day the glass pond was moved into the conservatory, "to be out of the way." The fish were excellent eating, and though the snails were at their wits' end as the refuse rotted, and the water became more stagnant, and the weeds grew, till all the shell-fish in the pond could not have kept the place clean,—I did not mind it myself. As the water got low, I found a nice bit of rockwork above water, where I could sit by day, and at night the lights from the drawing-room gave an indescribable stimulus to my wings, and I sailed in, and flew round and round till I was tired, and (forgetting that no pond, not even a bed of mud, was below me!) drew in my wings, and dropped sharply down on to the floor. To do the family justice, they learned to know the sound of my fall, and even the old Doctor himself would go down on hands and knees to hunt for me under the sofa, for fear I should be trodden on.

On the fifth day I swallowed the scarlet spider. I hated myself for doing it, when I thought of Molly; but the spider was very foolish to meet me. He should have kept behind. And if I hadn't eaten him, the dragon-fly larva would. What *he* had eaten, I do not think he could have told himself. There was very little left now for any one; even the water-scorpion had disappeared.

On the sixth day the glass pond had only two tenants worth speaking of—the dragon-fly larva and myself. We had both over-eaten ourselves, and for some hours we moved slowly about through the thickening puddle, nodding civilly when we passed each other among the feathery sprays of the Water Crowfoot. Then I began to get hungry. I knew it by feeling an impulse to look out for the dragon-fly larva, and I knew he knew it because he began to avoid me.

On the seventh day Molly ran into the conservatory, followed by her brother, and uttered a cry of dismay.

"Oh, what a state it's in! Where are the syphons?"

"Why, they melted the day Edward Brown came back. We've been having such a lot of cricket, Molly!"

"There isn't a fish left, and it smells horribly."

"I'm very sorry, Molly. Let's throw it out. I don't want Grandfather to see it. Let me come."

"No, no, Francis! There may be some left. Yes, there's the beetle. I shall put it all in a pail and take it back to the pond. Oh dear! oh dear! I can't see anything of the scarlet spider. My beautiful scarlet spider! I was so fond of him. Oh, I am so sorry! And no one has watered the Soldier, and he's dead too."

"Don't cry, Molly! Please don't cry! I dare say the spider is there, only it's so small."

For some time Molly poked carefully here and there, but the spider was not to be found, and the contents of the aquarium were carried back to the wood.

I was very glad to see the pond again. The water-gnats were taking dimensions as usual, a blue-black beetle sat humming on the stake, and dragon-flies flitted hungrily about, like splinters of a broken rainbow; but the Water-Soldier's place was empty, and it was never refilled. He was the only specimen.

Molly was probably in the right when, after a last vain search for the scarlet spider, as Francis slowly emptied the pail, she said with a sigh,

"What makes me so very sorry is, that I don't think we ought to have 'collected' things unless we had really attended to them, and knew how to keep them alive."

FOOTNOTES:

Footnote D: Water-soldier—*Stratiotes aloides.* A handsome and rare plant, of aloe-like appearance, with a white blossom rising in the centre of its sword-leaves.

AMONG THE MERROWS

A SKETCH OF A GREAT AQUARIUM

I remember the time when I, and a brother who was with me, devoutly believed in a being whom we supposed to live among certain black, water-rotted, weed-grown stakes by the sea. These old wooden ruins were, I fancy, the remains of some rude pier, and amid them, when the tide was low, we used to play, and to pay fancy visits to our fancy friend.

We called her Shriny—why, I know no more than when I first read Croker's delightful story of "The Soul Cages" I knew why the Merrow whom Jack went to see below the waves was called Coomara.

My remembrance of even what we fancied about Shriny is very dim now; and as my brother was only four years old (I was eight), his is not more distinct. I know we thought of her, and talked of her, and were always eager to visit her supposed abode, and wander together amongst its rotten pillars (which, as we were so small, seemed lofty enough in our eyes), where the mussels and limpets held tightly on, and the slimy, olive-green fucus hung loosely down—a sea-ivy covering ruins made by the waves.

I have never been to the place since those days. If Shriny's

Juliana Horatia Ewing

palace is there now at all, I dare say I should find the stakes to be stumps, and all the vastness and mystery about them gone for ever. And yet we used to pretend to feast with her there. We served up the seed-vessels of the fucus as fish. I do not think we really ate them, we only sucked out the salt water, and tried to fancy we were enjoying the repast. Once we *began* to eat a limpet!—Beyond that point my memory is dumb.

I wonder how we should have felt if Shriny had really appeared to us, as Coomara appeared to Jack Dogherty, and taken us down below the waves, or kept us among the stakes of her palace till the tide flooded them, and perhaps filled it with wonderful creatures and beautiful things, and floated out the dank, dripping fucus into a veil of lace above our heads; as our mother used to float out little dirty lumps of seaweed into beautiful web-like pictures when she was preserving them for her collection.

Shriny never did come, though Mr. Croker says Coomara came to Jack.

Perhaps, young readers, some of you have never read the story of the Soul Cages. It is a long one, and I am not going to repeat it here, only to say a word or two about it, for which I have a reason.

Jack Dogherty—so the story goes—had always longed to see a Merrow. Merrow is the Irish name for seafolk; indeed, it properly means a mermaid. And Jack, you know, lived in a fairy tale, and not in lodgings at a watering-place on the south coast; so he saw his Merrow, though we never saw Shriny.

I do not think any of the after-history of the Merrow is equal to Mr. Croker's account of his first appearance to Jack:

afterwards "Old Coo" becomes more like a tipsy old fisherman than the man-fish that he was.

The first appearance was on the coast to the northward, when "just as Jack was turning a point, he saw something, like to nothing he had ever seen before, perched upon a rock at a little distance out to sea; it looked green in the body, as well as he could discern at that distance, and he would have sworn, only the thing was impossible, that it had a cocked-hat in its hand. Jack stood for a good half-hour, straining his eyes and wondering at it, and all the time the thing did not stir hand or foot. At last Jack's patience was quite worn out, and he gave a loud whistle and a hail, when the Merrow (for such it was) started up, put the cocked-hat on its head, and dived down, head foremost, from the rocks."

For a long time Jack could get no nearer view of "the sea-gentleman with the cocked-hat," but at last, one stormy day, when he had taken refuge in one of the caves along the coast, "he saw, sitting before him, a thing with green hair, long green teeth, a red nose, and pig's eyes. It had a fish's tail, legs with scales on them, and short arms like fins. It wore no clothes, but had the cocked-hat under its arm, and seemed engaged thinking very seriously about something."

As I copy these words—*It wore no clothes, but had the cocked-hat under its arm, and seemed engaged thinking very seriously about something*—it seems to me that the portrait is strangely like something that I have seen. And the more I think of it, the more I am convinced that the type is familiar to me, and that, though I do not live in a fairy story, I have been among the Merrows. And further still that any one who pleases may go and see Coomara's cousins any day.

There can be no doubt of it! I have seen a Merrow—several Merrows. That unclothed, over-harnessed form is before me

Juliana Horatia Ewing

now; sitting motionless on a rock, "engaged thinking very seriously," till in some sudden impulse it rises, turns up its red nose, makes some sharp angular movements with head and elbows, and plunges down, with about as much grace as if some stiff, red-nosed old admiral, dressed in nothing but cocked-hat, spectacles, telescope, and a sword between his legs, were to take a header from the quarter-deck into the sea.

I do not want to make a mystery about nothing. I should have resented it thoroughly myself when I was young. I make no pretence to have had any glimpses of fairyland. I could not see Shriny when I was eight years old, and I never shall now. Besides, no one sees fairies now-a-days. The "path to bonnie Elfland" has long been overgrown, and few and far between are the Princes who press through and wake the Beauties that sleep beyond. For compensation, the paths to Mother Nature's Wonderland are made broader, easier, and more attractive to the feet of all men, day by day. And it is Mother Nature's Merrows that I have seen—in the Crystal Palace Aquarium.

How Mr. Croker drew that picture of Coomara the Merrow, when he probably never saw a sea crayfish, a lobster, or even a prawn at home, I cannot account for, except by the divining and prophetic instincts of genius. And when I speak of his seeing a crayfish, a lobster, or a prawn at home, I mean at their home, and not at Mr. Croker's. Two very different things for our friends the "sea-gentlemen," as to colour as well as in other ways. In his own home, for instance, a lobster is of various beautiful shades of blue and purple. In Mr. Croker's home he would be bright scarlet—from boiling! So would the prawn, and as solid as you please; who in his own home is colourless and transparent as any ghost.

Strangely beautiful those prawns are when you see them at

home. And that one seems to do in the Great Aquarium; though, I suppose, it is much like seeing land beasts and birds in the Zoological Gardens—a poor imitation of their free life in their natural condition. Still, there is no other way in which you can see and come to know these wonderful "sea gentlemen" so well, unless you could go, like Jack Dogherty, to visit them at the bottom of the sea. And whilst I heartily recommend every one who has not seen the Aquarium to visit it as soon as possible, let me describe it for the benefit of those who cannot do so at present. It may also be of some little use to them hereafter to know what is most worth seeing there, and where to look for it.

No sooner have you paid your sixpence at the turnstile which admits you, than your eye is caught by what seems to be a large window in the wall, near the man who has taken your money. You look through the glass, and find yourself looking into a deep sea-pool, with low stone-grey rocks studded with sea-anemones in full bloom. There are twenty-one different species of sea-anemones in the Aquarium; but those to be seen in this particular pool are chosen from about seven of the largest kinds. The very biggest, a *Tealia crassicornis*, measures ten inches across when he spreads his pearly fingers to their full extent. "In my young days" we called him by the familiar name of Crassy; and found him so difficult to keep in domestic captivity, that it was delightful to see him blooming and thriving as he does in Tank No. 1 of the Great Aquarium. His squat build—low and broad—contrasts well with those tall white neighbours of his (*Dianthus plumosa*), whose faces are like a plume of snowy feathers. All the sea-anemones in this tank have settled themselves on the rocks according to their own fancy. They are of lovely shades of colour, rosy, salmon-coloured, and pearly-white.

There are more than five thousand sea-anemones of various

Juliana Horatia Ewing

kinds in the Aquarium; and they have an attendant, whose sole occupation is to feed them, by means of a pair of long wooden forceps.

Reluctantly breaking away from such old friends, we pass through a door into a long vault-like stone passage or hall, down one side of which there seem to be high large windows, about as far apart as windows of a long room commonly are. Behind each of these is a sea-pool like the first one.

Take the first of the lot—Tank No. 2. It is stocked with *Serpulae*. Sea-anemones are well-known to most people, but tube-worms are not such familiar friends; so I will try to describe this particular kind of "sea-gentlemen." The tube-worms are so called because, though they are true worms (sea-worms), they do not trust their soft bodies to the sea, as our common earth-worms trust theirs in a garden-bed, but build themselves tubes inside which they live, popping their heads out at the top now and then like a chimney-sweep pushing his brush out at the top of a tall round chimney. Now if you can fancy one of our tall round manufactory chimneys to be white instead of black, and the round chimney-sweep's brush to have lovely gay-coloured feathers all round it instead of dirty bristles, or if you can fancy the sweep letting off a monster catherine-wheel at the chimney's mouth, you may have some idea what a tube-worm's head is like when he pokes it out of his tube.

The *Serpulae* make their tubes of chalky stuff, something like egg-shell; and they stick them on to anything that comes to hand down below. Those in the Great Aquarium came from Weymouth. They were dredged up with the white pipes or tubes sticking to oyster-shells, old bottles, stones, and what not, like bits of maccaroni glued on to old crockery sherds. These odds and ends are overgrown, however, with weeds and zoophytes, and (like an ugly house covered by creepers) look picturesque rather than otherwise. The worms have small bristles down their bodies, which serve as feet, and help them to scramble up inside their tubes, when they wish to poke their heads out and breathe. These heads are delicate, bright-coloured plumes. Each species has its own plume of its own special shape and colour. They are only to be seen when the animal is alive. A good many little *Serpulae* have been born in the Aquarium.

Through the next window—Tank No. 3—you may see more tube-worms, with ray-like, daisy heads, and soft muddy tubes. They are *Sabellae*.

Have you ever see a "sea-mouse"? Probably you have: preserved in a bottle. It is only like a mouse from being about the size of a mouse's body, without legs, and with a lot of rainbow-coloured hairs. You may be astonished to hear that it is classed among the worms. There is a sea-mouse in the Great Aquarium. I did not see him; perhaps because he is given to burrowing. If he is not in one of the two tanks just named he is probably in No. 21 or No. 25. He is so handsome dead and in a bottle, that he must be gorgeous to behold alive and in a pool. You should look out for him.

It is a disappointing feature of this water wonderland that some of the "sea-gentlemen" are apt to hide, like hobble-dehoy children, when visitors call. Indeed, a good many of them—such as the swimming-crabs, the burrowing-crabs, the sea-scorpions, and the eels—are night-feeders, and one cannot expect them to change their whole habits and customs to be seen of the British public. Anyhow, whether they hide from custom or caprice, they are quite safe from interference. Much happier, in this respect, than the beasts in the Zoological Gardens. One may disturb the big elephant's repose with umbrella-points, or throw buns at the brown bear, but the "sea-gentlemen" are safe in their caves, and humanity flattens its nose against the glass wall of separation in vain.

When I looked into Tank No. 5, however, there were several swimming-crabs and sea-scorpions to be seen. The sea-scorpions are fish, but bold-faced, fiery, greedy little fellows. The swimming-crabs are said to be "the largest, strongest, and *hungriest*" of English crabs. What a thought for those they live on! Let us picture to ourselves the largest, strongest, and *hungriest* of cannibals! Doubtless he would make short work even of the American Giant, as the swimming-crabs, by night, devour other crabs, larger but milder-tempered than themselves. It speaks volumes for the sea-scorpions, who are small fish, that they can hold their own in the same pool with the swimming-crabs.

Tank 4 contains big spider-crabs, who sit with their knees above their heads, winking at you with their eyes and feelers; or scramble out unexpectedly from dens and caves here and there, high up in the rocky sides of the pool.

Nos. 6, 7, and 8 contain fish.

It really is sad to think how completely our ideas on the subject of cod spring from the kitchen and the fish-kettle. (As to our cod-liver oil, we know no more how much of it has anything to do with cod-fish than we can guess where our milk and port-wine come from.) Poor cod! If of a certain social standing, it's odds if we will recognize any of him but his head and shoulders. I have seen him served up in country inns with a pickled walnut in the socket of each eye; and in life, and at home, he has the attentive, inquisitive, watchful, humorous eyes common to all fishes.

Fishes remind me rather of Chinese, who are also a

cold-blooded race: slow, watchful, inquisitive, acquisitive, and full of the sense of humour. There are fishes in the Great Aquarium whose faces twinkle again with quiet fun.

The cod here seemed quite as much interested in looking at us through a glass window as we were in looking at them. They are tame, and have very large appetites—so tame, and so hungry, that the fish who live with them are at a disadvantage at meal-times, and it is feared that they must be removed.

These other fish are plaice, soles, brill, turbot, and skate. The skate love to lie buried over head and ears in the sand. The faintest outline of tail or a flapping fin betrays the spot, and you long for an umbrella-poke from some Zoological-Garden-frequenting old lady, to stir the lazy creature up; but it is impossible.

Suddenly, when you are as tired of waiting as Jack was when Coomara was "engaged thinking," the fin movement becomes more distinct, a cloud of sand rises into the water, and a grey-coated skate, with two ornamental knobs upon his tail, flaps slowly away across the pool.

Sometimes these flat-fish flap upwards to the surface, poke their noses into the other world, and then, like larks, having gone up with effort, let themselves easily down again to the ground.

As we were looking into No. 7, an ambitious little sole took into his head to climb up the rocks, in the caves of which dwell crusty crabs. By marvellously agile doubles of his flat little body, he scrambled a good way up. Then he fell, and two or three valiant efforts still proving vain, he gave it up.

"He's turned giddy!" shouted a man beside us, who, like

Juliana Horatia Ewing

every one else, was watching the sea-gentlemen with rapt interest.

Why the little sole tried rock climbing I don't know, and I doubt if he knew himself.

Tank 7 is full of Basse—glittering fish who keep their silver armour clean by scrubbing it among the stones. Like other prettily-dressed people, they look out of the window all along.

At Tanks 1, 2, and 3, your chief feelings will be curiosity and admiration. The sea-flowers and the worms are rather low in the scale of living things. Far be it from you to decide that there are any living creatures with whom a loving and intelligent patience will not at last enable us to hold communion. But though, when you put the point of your little finger towards a Crassy, he gives it a very affectionate squeeze, and seems rather anxious to detain it permanently, the balance of evidence favours the idea that his appetite rather than his affections are concerned, and that he has only mistaken you for his dinner.

At present our intercourse is certainly limited, and though the *Serpulae* and *Sabellae* have their heads out of their chimneys all along, there is no reason to suppose that they take the slightest interest in the human beings who peer at them through the glass.

But with the fishes it is quite another thing. When you can fairly look into eyes as bright and expressive as your own, a long stride has been taken towards friendly relations. You flatten your nose on one side of the glass, and Mr. Fish flattens his on the other. If you have the stoniest of British stares he will outstare you. You long to scratch his back, or show him some similar attention, and (if he be a cod) to ask him, as between friends, why on earth (I mean in sea) he wears that queer horn under his chin.

Now with the *Crustaceans*(hard-shelled sea-gentlemen) it is different again. So far as one feels friendly towards a fish it is a fellow feeling. You know people like this or that cod, as one knows people like certain sheep, dogs, and horses. And a very short acquaintance with fish convinces you that not only is there a type of face belonging to each species, but that individual countenances vary, as with us. It is said that shepherds know the faces of their sheep as well as of their other friends, and I have no doubt that the keeper of the Great Aquarium knows his cod apart quite well.

And if one's feeling for the *Crustaceans*—the crabs, lobsters, prawns, &c.—is different, it is not because one feels them to be less intelligent than fishes, but because their intelligence is altogether a mysterious, unfathomable, unmeasurable quantity. There's no saying what they don't know. There is no telling how much they can see. And the great puzzle is what they can be thinking of. For that the spiny lobsters are thinking, and "thinking very seriously about something," you can no more doubt than Jack did about the Merrow.

The spiny lobsters (commonly, but erroneously called crawfish or cray-fish) and the common lobsters are in Tank No. 9.

Ah! that is a wonderful pool. The first glimpse of the spiny lobsters is enough for any one who has read of Coomara. We are among the Merrows at last.

I don't know that Coomara was a lobster, but I think he must have been a crustacean. Even his green hair reminds one of the spider-crabs; though matter-of-fact naturalists tell us that *their* green hair is only seaweed which grows luxuriantly on their shells from their quiet habits, and because they are not given to burrowing, or cleaning themselves among the stones like the silver-coated basse. At one time, by the bye, it was supposed that they dressed themselves in weeds, whence they were called "vanity-crabs."

But the spiny lobsters—please to look at them, and see if you can so much as guess their age, their capabilities, or their intentions. I fancy that the difference between the feelings with which they and the fishes inspire us is much the same as that between our mental attitude towards hill-men or house-elves, and towards men and women.

The spiny lobsters are red. The common lobsters are blue. The spiny lobsters are large, their eyes are startlingly prominent, their powerful antennae are longer and redder than Coomara's nose, and wave about in an inquisitive and somewhat threatening manner. When four or five of them are gathered together in the centre of the pool, sitting solemnly on their tails, which are tucked neatly under them, each with his ten sharp elbows a-kimbo "engaged thinking" (and perhaps talking) "very seriously about something," it is an impressive but *uncanny* sight.

We witnessed such a conclave, sitting in a close circle, face to face, waving their long antennae; and as we watched, from the shadowy caves above another merrow appeared. How he ever got his cumbersome coat of mail, his stiff legs, and long spines safely down the face of the cliff is a mystery. But he scrambled down ledge by ledge, bravely, and in some haste. He knew what the meeting was about, though we did not, and soon took his place, arranged his tail, his scales, his elbows, his cocked-hat, and what not, and fell a-thinking, like the rest. We left them so.

Most of the common lobsters were in their caves, from which they watched this meeting of the reds with fixed attention.

In their dark-blue coats, peering with their keen eyes from behind jutting rocks and the mouths of sea caverns, they looked somewhat like smuggler sailors!

Tanks 10 to 13 have fish in them. The Wrasses are very beautiful in colour. Most gorgeous indeed, if you can look at them in a particular way. Tank 32 has been made on purpose to display them. It is in another room.

No tank in the Aquarium is more popular than Tank 14. Enthusiastic people will sit down here with needlework or luncheon, and calmly wait for a good view of—the cuttle-fish!

Cuttle is the name for the whole race of cephalopods, and is supposed to be a corruption of the word cuddle, in the sense of hugging.

They are curious creatures, the one who favoured us with a good view of him being very like a loose red velvet pincushion with eight legs, and most of the bran let out.

Yet this strange, unshapely creature has a distinct brain in a soft kind of skull, mandibles like a parrot, and plenty of sense. His sight, hearing, touch, taste, and smell are acute. He lies kicking his legs in the doorway of his favourite cavern, which he selected for himself and is attached to, for a provokingly long time before he will come out. When he does appear, a subdued groan of gratified expectation runs through the crowd in front of his window, as head over heels, hand over hand, he sprawls downwards, and moves quickly away with the peculiar gait induced by having suckers instead of feet to walk with.

Juliana Horatia Ewing

Tank 15 contains eels. It seems to be a curious fact that fresh-water eels will live in sea-water. I should think, when they have once got used to the salt, they must find a pond very tasteless afterwards. They are night-feeders, as school-boys know well.

Tank 16. Fish—grey mullet. Tank 17. Prawns.

If with the fishes we had felt with friends, and with the lobsters as if with hobgoblins, with the prawns we seemed to find ourselves among ghosts.

A tank that seems only a pool for a cuttle-fish, or a cod, is a vast region where prawns and shrimps are the inhabitants. The caves look huge, and would hold an army of them. The rocks jut boldly out, and throw strange shadows on the pool. The light falls effectively from above, and in and out and round about go the prawns, with black eyes glaring from their diaphanous helmets, in colourless, translucent, if not transparent armour, and bristling with spears.

"They are like disembodied spirits," said my husband.

But in a moment more we exclaimed, "It's like a scene from Martin's mezzo-tint illustrations of the *Paradise Lost*. They are ghostly hosts gathering for battle."

This must seem a most absurd idea in connection with prawns; but if you have never seen prawns except at the breakfast-table, you must go to the Great Aquarium to learn how impressive is their appearance in real life.

The warlike group which struck us so forcibly had gathered rapidly from all parts of the pool upon a piece of flat table-rock that jutted out high up. Some unexplained excitement agitated the host; their innumerable spear-like antennae moved ceaselessly. From above a ray of light fell just upon the table-rock where they were gathered, making the waving spears glitter like the bayonet points of a body of troops, and forming a striking contrast with the dark cliffs and overshadowed water below, from which stragglers were quickly gathering, some paddling across the deep pool, others scrambling up the rocks, and all with the same fierce and restless expression.

How I longed for a chance of sketching the scene!

Prawns are not quite such colourless creatures in the sea as they are here. Why they lose their colour and markings in captivity is not known. They seem otherwise well.

They are hungry creatures, and their scent is keen.

The shrimps keep more out of sight; they burrow in the sand a good deal. You know one has to look for fresh-water shrimps in a brook if one wants to find them.

In Tank 18 are our old friends the hermit-crabs. As a child, I think I believed that these curious creatures killed the original inhabitants of the shells which they take for their own dwelling. It is pleasant to know that this is not the case. The hermit-crab is in fact a sea-gentleman, who is so unfortunate as to be born naked, and quite unable to make his own clothes, and who goes nervously about the world, trying on other people's cast-off coats till he finds one to fit him.

They are funnily fastidious about their shells, feeling one well inside and out before they decide to try it, and hesitating sometimes between two, like a lady between a couple of becoming bonnets. They have been said to be pugnacious; but I fancy that the old name of soldier-crabs was given to

Juliana Horatia Ewing

them under the impression that they killed the former proprietors of their shells.

With No. 18 the window tanks come to an end.

In two other rooms are a number of shallow tanks open at the top, in which are smaller sea-anemones, star-fish, more crabs, fishes, &c., &c.

Blennies are quaint, intellectual-looking little fish; friendly too, and easy to be tamed. In one of Major Holland's charming papers in *Science Gossip* he speaks of a pet blenny of his who was not only tame but musical. "He was exceedingly sensitive to the vibrations of stringed instruments; the softest note of a violin threw him into a state of agitation, and a harsh scrape or a vigorous *staccato* drove him wild."

In Tank 34 are gurnards, fish-gentlemen, with exquisite blue fins, like peacock's feathers.

No. 35 contains dragonets and star-fish. The dragonets are quaint, wide-awake little fish. I saw one snap at a big, fat, red star-fish, who was sticking to the side of a rock. Why the dragonet snapped at him I have no idea. I do not believe he hurt him; but the star-fish gradually relaxed his hold, and fell slowly and helplessly on to his back; on which the dragonet looked as silly as the Sultan of Casgar's purveyor when the hunchback fell beneath his blows. Another dragonet came hastily up to see what was the matter; but prudently made off again, and left the star-fish and his neighbour as they were. I waited a long time by the tank, watching for the result; but in vain. The star-fish, looking abjectly silly, lay with his white side up, without an effort to help himself. As to the dragonet, he stuck out his nose, fixed his eyes, and fell a-thinking. So I left them.

In Tank 38 are some Norwegian lobsters; red and white, very pretty, and differing from the English ones in form as well as colour.

The green anemones in Tank 33 are very beautiful.

The arrangement of most of these tanks is temporary. As some sea-gentlemen are much more rapacious than others, and as some prey upon others, the arranging of them must have been very like the old puzzle of the fox, the goose, and the bag of seed. Then when new creatures arrive it necessitates fresh arrangements.

There is not much vegetation as yet in the tanks, which may puzzle some people who have been accustomed to balance the animal and vegetable life in their aquaria by introducing full-grown sea-weeds. But it has been found that these often fail, and that it is better to trust to the weeds which come of themselves from the action of light upon the invisible seeds which float in all sea-water.

The pools are also kept healthy by the water being kept in constant motion through the agency of pipes, steam-engines, and a huge reservoir of sea-water.

It is not easy to speak with due admiration of the scientific skill, the loving patience, the mindfulness of the public good which must have gone to the forming of this Public Aquarium. With what different eyes must innumerable "trippers" from the less-educated masses of our people look into tide pools or crab holes, during their brief holiday at the seaside, if they have previously been "trippers" to the Crystal Palace, and visited the Great Aquarium.

Let us hope that it may stir up some sight-seers to be naturalists, and some naturalists to devote their powers to

Juliana Horatia Ewing

furthering our too limited friendship with the sea-gentry. How much remains to be done may be gathered from the fact that we can as yet keep no deep-sea Merrows in aquaria, only shore-dwellers will live with us, and not all of these. And so insuperable, as yet, are the difficulties of transport, that "distinguished foreigners" are rare indeed.

Still, as it stands, this Great Aquarium is wonderful—wonderful exceedingly. There is a still greater one at Brighton, holding greater wonders—a baby alligator amongst them—and we are very glad to hear that one is to be established in Manchester also.

It has been well said that a love of nature is a strong characteristic even of the roughest type of Britons. An Englishman's first idea of a holiday is to get into the country, even if his second is apt to be a search for the country beer-house.

Of birds, and beasts, and trees, and flowers, there is a good deal even of rustic lore. Of the wonders of the deep we know much less.

Thousands of us can sing with understanding,

    O Lord, how manifold are thy works!
    In wisdom hast thou made them all.
    The earth is full of Thy riches.

Surely hereafter more of us shall swell the antiphon,

    So is the great and wide sea also,
    Wherein are things creeping innumerable,
    Both small and great beasts.

*   *   *   *   *

NOTE.—A Great Aquarium (and something more) is being made at Naples by a young German naturalist—Dr. Dohrn, of Stettin—at an expense of between L7000 and L8000, nearly all of which comes out of his own pocket. The ground-floor of the building (an area of nearly eight thousand square feet) is to hold the Great Aquarium. It is hoped that the money obtained by opening this to the public will both support the Aquarium itself, and do something towards defraying the expenses of the upper story of the Zoological Station, as it is called. This will contain a scientific library, including Dr. Dohrn's own valuable private collection, and tables for naturalists to work at, furnished with necessary appurtenances, including tanks supplied with a constant stream of sea-water. Sea-fishing and dredging will be carried on in connection with the establishment, to supply subjects for study. Dr. Dohrn proposes to let certain of these tables to governments and scientific societies, who will then have the privilege of giving certificates, which will enable their naturalists to enjoy all the benefits of the institution.

Surely some new acquaintances will be made among the sea-gentry in this paradise of naturalists!

Juliana Horatia Ewing

TINY'S TRICKS AND TOBY'S TRICKS

TINY

"Oh Toby, my dear old Toby, you portly and princely Pug!

"You know it's bad for you to lie in the fender:—Father says that's what makes you so fat—and I want you to come and sit with me on the Kurdistan rug.

"Put your lovely black nose in my lap, and I'll count your great velvet wrinkles, and comfort you with kisses.

"If you'll only keep out of the fender—Father says you'll have a fit if you don't!—and give good advice to your poor Little Missis.

"Father says you are the wisest creature he knows, and you are but eight years old, and three months ago I was six.

"And yet Mother says I'm the silliest little girl that she ever met with, because I am always picking up tricks.

"She does not know where I learnt to stand on one leg (unless it was from a goose), but it has made one of my shoulders stick out more than the other.

"It wasn't the goose who taught me to whistle up and down-stairs. I learnt that last holidays from my brother.

"The baker's man taught me to put my tongue in my cheek when I'm writing copies, for I saw him do it when he was receipting a bill.

"And I learnt to wrinkle my forehead, and squeeze up my eyes, and make faces with my lips by imitating the strange doctor who attended us when we were ill.

"It was Brother Jack himself who showed me that the way to squint is to look at both sides of your nose.

"And then, Toby—would you believe it?—he turned round last holidays and said—'Look here, Tiny, if the wind changes when you're making that face it'll stay there, and remember you can't squint properly and keep your eye on the weathercock at the same time to see how it blows.'"

"But boys are so mean!—and I catch stammering from his school friend—'*Tut-tut-tut-tut-Tom*,' as we call him—but I soon leave it off when he goes."

"I did not learn stooping and poking out my chin from any one; it came of itself. It is so hard to sit up; but Mother says that much my worst trick."

"Is biting my finger nails; and I've bitten them nearly all down to the quick."

"She says if I don't lose these tricks, and leave off learning fresh ones, I shall never grow up like our pretty great-great-grandmamma."

"Do you know her, dear Toby? I don't think you do. I don't

Juliana Horatia Ewing

think you ever look at pictures, intelligent as you are!"

"It's the big portrait, by Romney, of a beautiful lady, sitting beautifully up, with her beautiful hands lying in her lap."

"Looking over her shoulder, out of lovely eyes, with a sweet smile on her lips, in the old brocade Mother keeps in the chest, and a pretty lace cap."

"I should very much like to be like her when I grow up to that age; Mother says she was twenty-six."

"And of course I know she would not have looked so nice in her picture if she'd squinted, and wrinkled her forehead, and had one shoulder out, and her tongue in her cheek, and a round back, and her chin poked, and her fingers all swollen with biting;—but, oh, Toby, you clever Pug! how am I to get rid of my tricks?"

"That is, if I must give them up; but it seems so hard to get into disgrace."

"For doing what comes natural to one, with one's own eyes, and legs, and fingers, and face."

TOBY.

"Remove your arms from my neck, Little Missis—I feel unusually apoplectic—and let me take two or three turns on the rug."

"Whilst I turn the matter over in my mind, for never was there so puzzled a Pug!"

"I am, as your respected Father truly observes, a most talented creature."

"And as to fit subjects for family portraits and personal appearance—from the top of my massive brow to the tip of my curly tail, I believe myself to be perfect in every feature."

"And when my ears are just joined over my forehead like a black velvet cap, I'm reckoned the living likeness of a late eminent divine and once popular preacher."

"Did your great-great-grandmamma ever take a prize at a show? But let that pass—the real question is this:

"How is it that what I am most highly commended for, should in your case be taken amiss?"

"Why am I reckoned the best and cleverest of dogs? Because I've picked up tricks so quickly ever since I was a pup."

"And if I couldn't wrinkle my forehead and poke out my chin, and grimace at the judges, do you suppose I should ever have been—Class Pug. First Prize—Champion and Gold Cup?"

"We have one thing in common—I do *not* find it easy to sit up."

"But I learned it, and so will you. I can't imagine worse manners than to put one's tongue in one's cheek; as a rule, I hang mine gracefully out on one side."

"And I've no doubt it's a mistake to gnaw your fingers. I gnawed a good deal in my puppyhood, but chewing my paws is a trick that I never tried."

"How you stand on one leg I cannot imagine; with my figure it's all I can do to stand upon four."

"I balance biscuit on my nose. Do you? I jump through a hoop (an atrocious trick, my dear, after one's first youth—and a full meal!)—I bark three cheers for the Queen, and I shut the dining-room door."

"I lie flat on the floor at the word of command—In short, I've as many tricks as you have, and every one of them counts to my credit;

"Whilst yours—so you say—only bring you into disgrace, which I could not have thought possible if you had not said it."

"Indeed—but for the length of my experience and the solidity of my judgment—this would tempt me to think your mamma a very foolish person, and to advise you to disobey her; but I do *not*, Little Missis, for I know

"That if you belong to good and kind people, it is well to let them train you up in the way in which they think you should go."

"Your excellent parents trained me to tricks; and very senseless some of them seemed, I must say:"

"But I've lived to be proud of what I've been taught; and glad too that I learned to obey."

"For, depend upon it, if you never do as you're told till you know the reason why, or till you find that you must;"

"You are much less of a Prize Pug than you might have been if you'd taken good government on trust."

* * * * *

"Take me back to your arms, Little Missis, I feel cooler, and calmer in my mind."

"Yes, there can be no doubt about it. You must do what your mother tells you, for you know that she's wise and kind."

"You must take as much pains to *lose your* tricks as I took to *learn mine*, long ago;"

"And we may all live to see you yet—'Class, Young Lady. First Prize. Gold Medal—of a Show.'"

TINY.

"Oh, Toby, my dear old Toby, you wise and wonderful Pug!"

"Don't struggle off yet, stay on my knee for a bit, you'll be much hotter in the fender, and I want to give you a great, big hug."

"What are you turning round and round for? you'll make yourself giddy, Toby. If you're looking for your tail, it is there, all right."

"You can't see it for yourself because you're so fat, and because it is curled so tight."

"I dare say you could play with it, like Kitty, when you were a pup, but it must be a long time now since you've seen it."

"It's rather rude of you, Mr. Pug, to lie down with your back to me, and a grunt, but I know you don't mean it."

"I wanted to hug you, Toby, because I do thank you for giving me such good advice, and I know every word of it's true."

Juliana Horatia Ewing

"I mean to try hard to follow it, and I'll tell you what I shall do."

"Nurse wants to put bitter stuff on the tips of my fingers, to cure me of biting them, and now I think I shall let her."

"I know they're not fit to be seen, but she says they would soon become better."

"I mean to keep my hands behind my back a good deal till they're well, and to hold my head up, and turn out my toes; and every time I give way to one of my tricks, I shall go and stand (*on both legs*) before the picture, and confess it to great-great-grandmamma."

"Just fancy if I've no tricks left this time next year, Toby! Won't that show how clever we are?"

"I for trying so hard to do what I'm told, and you for being so wise that people will say—'That sensible pug cured that silly little girl when not even her mother could mend her.'"

"—Ah! Bad Dog! Where are you slinking off to?—Oh, Toby, darling! do, *do* take a little of your own good advice, and try to cure yourself of lying in the fender!"

THE OWL IN THE IVY BUSH;

OR,

THE CHILDREN'S BIRD OF WISDOM

INTRODUCTION.

"Hoot toots, man, yon's a queer bird!"

—Bonnie Scotland

I AM an Owl; a very fluffy one, in spite of all that that Bad Boy pulled out! I live in an Ivy Bush. Children are nothing to me, naturally, so it seems strange that I should begin, at my time of life, to observe their little ways and their humours, and to give them good advice.

And yet it is so. I am the Friend of Young People. In my flight abroad I watch them. As I sit meditating in my Ivy Bush, it is their little matters which I turn over in my fluffy head. I have established a letter-box for their communications at the Hole in the Tree. No other address will find me.

It is well known that I am a Bird of Wisdom. I am also an

Juliana Horatia Ewing

Observing Bird; and though my young friends may think I see less than I do, because of my blinking, and because I detest that vulgar glare of bright light without which some persons do not seem able to see what goes on around them, I would have children to know that if I can blink on occasion, and am not apt to let every starer read my counsel in my eyes, I am wide awake all the same. I am on the look-out when it's so dark that other folk can't see an inch before their noses, and (a word to the foolish and naughty!) I can see what is doing behind my back. And Wiseacre, Observer, and Wide-awake—I am the Children's Owl.

Before I open my mouth on their little affairs, before even I open my letters (if there are any waiting for me) I will explain how it came about that I am the Children's Owl.

It is all owing to that little girl; the one with the fluffy hair and the wise eyes. As an Observer I have noticed that not only I, but other people, seem to do what she wants, and as a Wiseacre I have reflected upon it as strange, because her temper is as soft and fluffy as her hair (which mine is not), and she always seems ready to give way to others (which is never my case—if I can help it). On the occasion I am about to speak of, I could *not* help it.

It was last summer that that Bad Boy caught me, and squeezed me into a wicker cage. Little did I think I should ever live to be so poked out, and rummaged, and torn to shreds by such a thing as a boy! I bit him, but he got me into the cage and put a cloth over it. Then he took me to his father, who took me to the front door of the house, where he is coachman and gardener, and asked for Little Miss to come out and see the new pet Tom had caught for her.

"It's a nasty-tempered brute, but she's such a one for taming things," said the coachman, whipping off the cloth to show me to the housemaid, and letting in a glare of light that irritated me to a frenzy. I flew at the housemaid, and she flew into the house. Then I rolled over and growled and hissed under my beak, and tried to hide my eyes in my feathers.

"Little Miss won't tame me," I muttered.

She did not try long. When she heard of me she came running out, the wind blowing her fluffy hair about her face, and the sun shining on it. Fluffed out by the wind, and changing colour in the light and shade, the hair down her back is not entirely unlike the feathers of my own, though less sober perhaps in its tints. Like mine it makes a small head look large, and as she had big wise eyes, I have seen creatures less like an owl than Little Miss. Her voice is not so hoarse as mine. It is clear and soft, as I heard when she spoke:

"Oh, *how* good of you! And how good of Tom! I do so love owls. I always get Mary to put the silver owl by me at luncheon, though I am not allowed to eat pepper. And I have a brown owl, a china one, sitting on a book for a letter weight. He came from Germany. And Captain Barton gave me an owl pencil-case on my birthday, because I liked hearing about his real owl, but, oh, I never hoped I should have a real owl of my very own. It *was* kind of Tom."

To hear that Bad Boy called kind was too much for endurance, and I let them see how savage I felt. If the wicker work had not been very strong the cage would not have held me.

"He's a Tartar," said the coachman.

"Oh no, Williams!" said Little Miss, "he's only frightened by

Juliana Horatia Ewing

the light. Give me the cloth, please."

"Take care, Miss. He'll bite you," cried the coachman, as she put the cloth over the cage, and then over her own head.

"No he won't! I don't mind his snapping and hissing. I want him to see me, and know me. Then perhaps he'll get to like me, and be tame, and sit on the nursery clock and look wise. Captain Barton's owl used to sit on his clock. Poor fellow! Dear old owlie! Don't growl, my owl. Can you hoot, darling? I should like to hear you hoot."

Sometimes as I sit in my Ivy Bush, and the moon shines on the spiders' webs and reminds me of the threads of her hair, on a mild, sleepy night, if there's nothing stirring but the ivy boughs; sitting, I say, blinking between a dream and a doze, I fancy I see her face close to mine, as it was that day with the wicker work between. Our eyes looking at each other, and our fluffiness mixed up by the wind. Then I try to remember all the kind things she said to me to coax me to leave my ivy bush, and go to live on the nursery clock. But I can't remember half. I was in such a rage at the time, and when you are in a rage you miss a good deal, and forget a good deal.

I know that at last she left off talking to me, and I could see her wise eyes swimming in tears. Then she left me alone under the cloth.

"Well, Miss," said the coachman, "you don't make much of him, do ye? He's a Tartar, Miss, I'm afraid."

"I think, Williams, that he's too old. Captain Barton's owl was a little owlet when he first got him. I shall never tame this one, Williams, and I never was so disappointed in all my life. Captain Barton said he kept an owl to keep himself good and wise, because nobody could be foolish in the face of an owl sitting on his clock. He says both his godfathers are dead, and he has taken his owl for his godfather. These are his jokes, Williams, but I had set my heart on having an owl on the nursery clock. I do think I have never wished so much for anything in the world as that Tom's owl would be our Bird of Wisdom. But he never will. He will never let me tame him. He wants to be a wild owl all his life. I love him very much, and I should like him to have what he wants, and not be miserable. Please thank Tom very much, and please ask him to let him go."

"I'm sorry I brought him, Miss, to trouble you," said the coachman. "But Tom won't let him go. He'd a lot of trouble catching him, and if he's no good to you, Tom'll be glad of him to stuff. He's got some glass eyes out of a stuffed fox the moths ate, and he's bent on stuffing an owl, is Tom. The eyes would be too big for a pheasant, but they'll look well enough in an owl, he thinks."

My hearing is very acute, and not a word of that Bad Boy's brutal intentions was lost on me. I shrunk among my feathers and shivered with despair; but when I heard the voice of Little Miss I rounded my ear once more.

"No, Williams, no! He must not be stuffed. Oh, please beg Tom to come to me. Perhaps I can give him something to persuade him not. If he must stuff an owl, please, please let him stuff a strange owl. One I haven't made friends with. Not this one. He is very wild, but he is very lovely and soft, and I do so want him to be let go."

"Well, Miss, I'll send Tom, and you can settle it with him. All I say, he's a Tartar, and stuffing's too good for him."

Whether she bribed Tom, or persuaded him, I don't know,

Juliana Horatia Ewing

but Little Miss got her way, and that Bad Boy let me go, and
I went back to my Ivy Bush.

OWLHOOT I

"What can't be cured must be endured."

—Old Proverb

It was the wish to see Little Miss once more that led my wings past her nursery window; besides, I had a curiosity to look at the clock.

It is an eight-day clock, in a handsome case, and would, undoubtedly, have been a becoming perch for a bird of my dignified appearance, but I will not describe it to-day. Nor will I speak of my meditations as I sit in my Ivy Bush like any other common owl, and reflect that if I had not had my own way, but had listened to Little Miss, I might have sat on an Eight-day Clock, and been godfather to the children. It is not seemly for an owl to doubt his own wisdom, but as I have taken upon me, for the sake of Little Miss, to be a child's counsellor, I will just observe, in passing, that though it is very satisfactory at the time to get your own way, you may live to wish that you had taken other folk's advice instead.

From that nursery I have taken flight to others. I sail by the windows, and throw a searching eye through these bars which are, I believe, placed there to keep top-heavy babies from tumbling out. Sometimes I peer down the chimney. From the nook of a wall or the hollow of a tree, I overlook the children's gardens and playgrounds. I have an eye to several schools, and I fancy (though I may be wrong) that I should look well seated on the top of an easel—just above the black-board, with a piece of chalk in my feathery foot.

Juliana Horatia Ewing

Not that I have any notion of playing school-master, or even of advising school-masters and parents how to make their children good and wise. I am the Children's Owl—their very own—and all my good advice is intended to help them to improve themselves.

It is wonderful how children *do* sometimes improve! I knew a fine little fellow, much made of by his family and friends, who used to be so peevish about all the little ups and downs of life, and had such a lamentable whine in his voice when he was thwarted in any trifle, that if you had heard without seeing him, you'd have sworn that the most miserable wretch in the world was bewailing the worst of catastrophes with failing breath. And all the while there was not a handsomer, healthier, better fed, better bred, better dressed, and more dearly loved little boy in all the parish. When you might have thought, by the sound of it, that some starving skeleton of a creature was moaning for a bit of bread, the young gentleman was only sobbing through the soap and lifting his voice above the towels, because Nurse would wash his fair rosy cheeks. And when cries like those of one vanquished in battle and begging and praying for his life, rang through the hall and up the front stairs, it proved to be nothing worse than Master Jack imploring his friends to "*please, please*" and "*do, do*," let him stay out to run in a final "go as you please" race with the young Browns (who dine a quarter of an hour later), instead of going in promptly when the gong sounded for luncheon.

Now the other day I peeped into a bedroom of that little boy's home. The sun was up, and so was Jack, but one of his numerous Aunts was not. She was in bed with a headache, and to this her pale face, her eyes shunning the light like my own, and her hair restlessly tossed over the pillow bore witness. When a knock came on the bedroom door, she started with pain, but lay down again and cried—"Come in!"

The door opened, but no one came in; and outside the voices of the little boy and his nurse were audible.

"I want to show her my new coat."

"You can't, Master Jack. Your Aunt's got a dreadful headache, and can't be disturbed."

No peevish complaints from Jack: only a deep sigh.

"I'm very sorry about her headache; and I'm very very sorry about my coat. For I am going out, and it will never be so new again."

His Aunt spoke feebly.

"Nurse, I must see his coat. Let him come in."

Enter Jack.

It was his first manly suit, and he was trying hard for a manly soul beneath it, as a brave boy should. He came in very gently, but with conscious pride glowing in his rosy cheeks and out of his shining eyes. His cheeks were very red, for a step in life is a warming thing, and so is a cloth suit when you've been used to frocks.

It was a bottle-green coat, with large mother-o'-pearl buttons and three coachman's capes; and there were leggings to match. The beaver hat, too, was new, and becomingly cocked, as he stood by his Aunt's bedside and smiled.

"What a fine coat, Jack!"

"Made by a tailor, Auntie Julie. Real pockets!"

"You don't say so!"

He nodded.

"Leggings too!" and he stuck up one leg at a sudden right angle on to the bed; a rash proceeding, but the boy has a straight little figure, and with a hop or two he kept his balance.

"My dear Jack, they are grand. How warm they must keep your legs!"

He shook his beaver hat.

"No. They only tickles. That's what they do."

There was a pause. His Aunt remembered the old peevish ways. She did not want to encourage him to discard his winter leggings, and was doubtful what to say. But in a moment more his eyes shone, and his face took that effulgent expression which some children have when they are resolved upon being good.

"—*and as I can't shake off the tickle, I have to bear it,*" added the little gentleman.

I call him the little gentleman advisedly. There is no stronger sign of high breeding in young people, than a cheerful endurance of the rubs of life. A temper that fits one's fate, a spirit that rises with the occasion. It is this kind of courage which the Gentlemen of England have shown from time immemorial, through peace and war, by land and sea, in every country and climate of the habitable globe. Jack is a child of that Empire on which the sun never sets, and if he live he is like to have larger opportunities of bearing discomfort than was afforded by the woolly worry of his bottle-green leggings. I am in good hopes that he will not be found wanting.

Some such thoughts, I believe, occurred to his Aunt.

"That's right, Jack. What a man you are!"

The rosy cheeks became carmine, and Jack flung himself upon his Aunt, and kissed her with resounding smacks.

A somewhat wrecked appearance which she presented after this boisterous hug, recalled the headache to his mind, and as he settled the beaver hat, which had gone astray, he said ruefully,

"Is your headache *very* bad, Auntie Julie?"

"Rather bad, Jack. *And as I can't shake if off, I have to bear it.*"

He went away on tiptoe, and it was only after he had carefully and gently closed the bedroom door behind him, that he departed by leaps and bounds to show himself in his bottle-green coat and capes, and white buttons and leggings to match, and beaver hat to boot, first to the young Browns, and after that to the General Public.

As an Observer, I may say that it was a sight worth seeing; and as a Bird of some wisdom, I prophesy well of that boy.

PROVERBS

Fine feathers make fine birds.

Manners make the man.

Juliana Horatia Ewing

Clowns are best in their own company; gentlemen are best everywhere.

Where there's a will there's a way.

All work and no play makes Jack a dull boy.

What can't be cured must be endured.

OWLHOOT II

"Then this ebony bird beguiling my sad fancy into smiling."

—The Raven

"Taffy was a thief."—*Old Song*

I find the following letters at the Hole in the Tree.

"X LINES, SOUTH CAMP, ALDERSHOT.

"SIR,—You speak with great feeling of that elevated position (I allude, of course, to the top of the eight-day clock), which circumstances led you somewhat hastily to decline. It would undoubtedly have become you, and less cannot be said for such a situation as the summit of an easel, overlooking the blackboard, in an establishment for the education of youth. Meanwhile it may interest you to hear of a bird (not of your wisdom, but with parts, and a respectable appearance) who secured a somewhat similar seat in adopting that kind of home which you would not. It was in driving through a wood at some little distance from the above address that we found a wounded crow, and brought him home to our hut. He became a member of the family, and received the name of Slyboots, for reasons with which it is unnecessary to trouble you. He was made very welcome in the drawing-room, but he preferred the kitchen. The kitchen is a brick room detached from the wooden hut. It was once, in fact, an armourer's shop, and has since been converted to a kitchen. The floor is rudely laid, and the bricks gape here and there. A barrack fender guards the fire-place, and a barrack poker reposes in the fender. It is a very ponderous poker of unusual size and the commonest appearance, but with a massive knob at the upper end which was wont to project far and high above the hearth. It was to this seat that Slyboots

Juliana Horatia Ewing

elevated himself by his own choice, and became the Kitchen Crow. Here he spent hours watching the cook, and taking titbits behind her back. He ate what he could (more, I fear, than he ought), and hid the rest in holes and corners. The genial neighbourhood of the oven caused him no inconvenience. His glossy coat, being already as black as a coal, was not damaged by a certain grimeyness which is undoubtedly characteristic of the (late) armourer's shop, of which the chimney is an inveterate smoker. Companies of his relatives constantly enter the camp by ways over which the sentries have no control (the Balloon Brigade being not yet even in the clouds); but Slyboots showed no disposition to join them. They flaunt and forage in the Lines, they inspect the ashpits and cookhouses, they wheel and manoeuvre on the parades, but Slyboots sat serene upon his poker. He had a cookhouse all to himself.... He died. We must all die; but we need not all die of repletion, which I fear, was his case. He buried his last meal between two bricks in the kitchen floor, and covered it very tidily with a bit of newspaper. The poker is vacant. Sir, I was bred to the sword and not to the pen, but I have a foolish desire for literary fame. I should be better pleased to be in print than to be promoted—for that matter one seems as near as the other—and my wife agrees with me. She is of a literary turn, and has helped me in the composition of this, but we both fear that the story having no moral you will not admit it into your Owlhoots. But if your wisdom could supply this, or your kindness overlook the defect, it would afford great consolation to a bereaved family to have printed a biography of the dear deceased. For we were greatly attached to him, though he preferred the cook. I can at any rate give you my word as a man of honour that these incidents are true, though, out of soldierly modesty, I will not trouble you with my name, but with much respect subscribe myself by that of

"SLYBOOTS."

The gallant officer is too modest. This biography is not only true but brief, and these are rare merits in a memoir. As to the moral—it is not far to seek. Dear children, for whom I hoot! avoid greediness. If Slyboots had eaten tit-bits in moderation, he might be sitting on the poker to this day. I have great pleasure in making his brief career public to the satisfaction of his gallant friend, and I should be glad to hear that the latter had got his step by the same post as his Owlhoot.

The second letter is much farther from literary excellence than the first. I fear this little boy plays truant from school as well as taking apples which do not belong to him. It is high time that he learnt to spell, and also to observe the difference between *meum* and *tuum*. From not being well grounded on these two points, many boys have lost good situations in life when they grew up to be men.

"deer mister howl,—as you say you see behind your bak i spose its you told varmer jones of me for theres a tree with a whole in it just behind the orchurd he wolloped I shameful and I'll have no more of his apples they be a deal sowerer than yud think though they look so red, but do you call yourself a childerns friend and tell tails i dont i can tell you.

"TOM TURNIP."

Juliana Horatia Ewing

ABOUT THE AUTHOR

Mrs. Juliana Horatia Ewing (née Gatty) (1841–1885) was a writer of children's stories, daughter of The Rev. Alfred Gatty and Margaret Gatty, also a writer for children. Among her tales, which have hardly been excelled in sympathetic insight into child-life, and still enjoy undiminished popularity, are: Mrs. Overtheway's Remembrances (1869), A Flat Iron for a Farthing (1872), Six to Sixteen (1875), Jan of the Windmill (1876), Jackanapes (1884), and The Story of a Short Life (1885).

Her works have been called the "first outstanding child-novels" in English literature.[1]

She was born at Ecclesfield, Yorkshire on August 3, 1841; married June 1, 1867, to Alexander Ewing and died at Bath, May 13, 1885. She was buried at Trull, Somerset, on May 16, 1885.

Other books by this author

A Flat Iron for a Farthing

A Great Emergency and Other Tales

Jan of the Windmill

Melchior's Dream and Other Tales

Miscellanea

Mrs. Overtheway's Remembrances

The Brownies and Other Tales

Juliana Horatia Ewing

Choose from Thousands of 1stWorldLibrary Classics By

A. M. Barnard
Ada Leverson
Adolphus William Ward
Aesop
Agatha Christie
Alexander Aaronsohn
Alexander Kielland
Alexandre Dumas
Alfred Gatty
Alfred Ollivant
Alice Duer Miller
Alice Turner Curtis
Alice Dunbar
Allen Chapman
Alleyne Ireland
Ambrose Bierce
Amelia E. Barr
Amory H. Bradford
Andrew Lang
Andrew McFarland Davis
Andy Adams
Angela Brazil
Anna Alice Chapin
Anna Sewell
Annie Besant
Annie Hamilton Donnell
Annie Payson Call
Annie Roe Carr
Annonaymous
Anton Chekhov
Archibald Lee Fletcher
Arnold Bennett
Arthur C. Benson
Arthur Conan Doyle
Arthur M. Winfield
Arthur Ransome
Arthur Schnitzler
Arthur Train
Atticus
B.H. Baden-Powell
B. M. Bower
B. C. Chatterjee
Baroness Emmuska Orczy
Baroness Orczy
Basil King
Bayard Taylor
Ben Macomber
Bertha Muzzy Bower
Bjornstjerne Bjornson

Booth Tarkington
Boyd Cable
Bram Stoker
C. Collodi
C. E. Orr
C. M. Ingleby
Carolyn Wells
Catherine Parr Traill
Charles A. Eastman
Charles Amory Beach
Charles Dickens
Charles Dudley Warner
Charles Farrar Browne
Charles Ives
Charles Kingsley
Charles Klein
Charles Hanson Towne
Charles Lathrop Pack
Charles Romyn Dake
Charles Whibley
Charles Willing Beale
Charlotte M. Braeme
Charlotte M. Yonge
Charlotte Perkins Stetson
Clair W. Hayes
Clarence Day Jr.
Clarence E. Mulford
Clemence Housman
Confucius
Coningsby Dawson
Cornelis DeWitt Wilcox
Cyril Burleigh
D. H. Lawrence
Daniel Defoe
David Garnett
Dinah Craik
Don Carlos Janes
Donald Keyhoe
Dorothy Kilner
Dougan Clark
Douglas Fairbanks
E. Nesbit
E. P. Roe
E. Phillips Oppenheim
E. S. Brooks
Earl Barnes
Edgar Rice Burroughs
Edith Van Dyne
Edith Wharton

Edward Everett Hale
Edward J. O'Biren
Edward S. Ellis
Edwin L. Arnold
Eleanor Atkins
Eleanor Hallowell Abbott
Eliot Gregory
Elizabeth Gaskell
Elizabeth McCracken
Elizabeth Von Arnim
Ellem Key
Emerson Hough
Emilie F. Carlen
Emily Bronte
Emily Dickinson
Enid Bagnold
Enilor Macartney Lane
Erasmus W. Jones
Ernie Howard Pie
Ethel May Dell
Ethel Turner
Ethel Watts Mumford
Eugene Sue
Eugenie Foa
Eugene Wood
Eustace Hale Ball
Evelyn Everett-green
Everard Cotes
F. H. Cheley
F. J. Cross
F. Marion Crawford
Fannie E. Newberry
Federick Austin Ogg
Ferdinand Ossendowski
Fergus Hume
Florence A. Kilpatrick
Fremont B. Deering
Francis Bacon
Francis Darwin
Frances Hodgson Burnett
Frances Parkinson Keyes
Frank Gee Patchin
Frank Harris
Frank Jewett Mather
Frank L. Packard
Frank V. Webster
Frederic Stewart Isham
Frederick Trevor Hill
Frederick Winslow Taylor

Friedrich Kerst
Friedrich Nietzsche
Fyodor Dostoyevsky
G.A. Henty
G.K. Chesterton
Gabrielle E. Jackson
Garrett P. Serviss
Gaston Leroux
George A. Warren
George Ade
Geroge Bernard Shaw
George Cary Eggleston
George Durston
George Ebers
George Eliot
George Gissing
George MacDonald
George Meredith
George Orwell
George Sylvester Viereck
George Tucker
George W. Cable
George Wharton James
Gertrude Atherton
Gordon Casserly
Grace E. King
Grace Gallatin
Grace Greenwood
Grant Allen
Guillermo A. Sherwell
Gulielma Zollinger
Gustav Flaubert
H. A. Cody
H. B. Irving
H. C. Bailey
H. G. Wells
H. H. Munro
H. Irving Hancock
H. R. Naylor
H. Rider Haggard
H. W. C. Davis
Haldeman Julius
Hall Caine
Hamilton Wright Mabie
Hans Christian Andersen
Harold Avery
Harold McGrath
Harriet Beecher Stowe
Harry Castlemon
Harry Coghill
Harry Houidini

Hayden Carruth
Helent Hunt Jackson
Helen Nicolay
Hendrik Conscience
Hendy David Thoreau
Henri Barbusse
Henrik Ibsen
Henry Adams
Henry Ford
Henry Frost
Henry James
Henry Jones Ford
Henry Seton Merriman
Henry W Longfellow
Herbert A. Giles
Herbert Carter
Herbert N. Casson
Herman Hesse
Hildegard G. Frey
Homer
Honore De Balzac
Horace B. Day
Horace Walpole
Horatio Alger Jr.
Howard Pyle
Howard R. Garis
Hugh Lofting
Hugh Walpole
Humphry Ward
Ian Maclaren
Inez Haynes Gillmore
Irving Bacheller
Isabel Cecilia Williams
Isabel Hornibrook
Israel Abrahams
Ivan Turgenev
J. G.Austin
J. Henri Fabre
J. M. Barrie
J. M. Walsh
J. Macdonald Oxley
J. R. Miller
J. S. Fletcher
J. S. Knowles
J. Storer Clouston
J. W. Duffield
Jack London
Jacob Abbott
James Allen
James Andrews
James Baldwin

James Branch Cabell
James DeMille
James Joyce
James Lane Allen
James Lane Allen
James Oliver Curwood
James Oppenheim
James Otis
James R. Driscoll
Jane Abbott
Jane Austen
Jane L. Stewart
Janet Aldridge
Jens Peter Jacobsen
Jerome K. Jerome
Jessie Graham Flower
John Buchan
John Burroughs
John Cournos
John F. Kennedy
John Gay
John Glasworthy
John Habberton
John Joy Bell
John Kendrick Bangs
John Milton
John Philip Sousa
John Taintor Foote
Jonas Lauritz Idemil Lie
Jonathan Swift
Joseph A. Altsheler
Joseph Carey
Joseph Conrad
Joseph E. Badger Jr
Joseph Hergesheimer
Joseph Jacobs
Jules Vernes
Julian Hawthrone
Julie A Lippmann
Justin Huntly McCarthy
Kakuzo Okakura
Karle Wilson Baker
Kate Chopin
Kenneth Grahame
Kenneth McGaffey
Kate Langley Bosher
Kate Langley Bosher
Katherine Cecil Thurston
Katherine Stokes
L. A. Abbot
L. T. Meade

L. Frank Baum
Latta Griswold
Laura Dent Crane
Laura Lee Hope
Laurence Housman
Lawrence Beasley
Leo Tolstoy
Leonid Andreyev
Lewis Carroll
Lewis Sperry Chafer
Lilian Bell
Lloyd Osbourne
Louis Hughes
Louis Joseph Vance
Louis Tracy
Louisa May Alcott
Lucy Fitch Perkins
Lucy Maud Montgomery
Luther Benson
Lydia Miller Middleton
Lyndon Orr
M. Corvus
M. H. Adams
Margaret E. Sangster
Margret Howth
Margaret Vandercook
Margaret W. Hungerford
Margret Penrose
Maria Edgeworth
Maria Thompson Daviess
Mariano Azuela
Marion Polk Angellotti
Mark Overton
Mark Twain
Mary Austin
Mary Catherine Crowley
Mary Cole
Mary Hastings Bradley
Mary Roberts Rinehart
Mary Rowlandson
M. Wollstonecraft Shelley
Maud Lindsay
Max Beerbohm
Myra Kelly
Nathaniel Hawthrone
Nicolo Machiavelli
O. F. Walton
Oscar Wilde
Owen Johnson
P.G. Wodehouse
Paul and Mabel Thorne

Paul G. Tomlinson
Paul Severing
Percy Brebner
Percy Keese Fitzhugh
Peter B. Kyne
Plato
Quincy Allen
R. Derby Holmes
R. L. Stevenson
R. S. Ball
Rabindranath Tagore
Rahul Alvares
Ralph Bonehill
Ralph Henry Barbour
Ralph Victor
Ralph Waldo Emmerson
Rene Descartes
Ray Cummings
Rex Beach
Rex E. Beach
Richard Harding Davis
Richard Jefferies
Richard Le Gallienne
Robert Barr
Robert Frost
Robert Gordon Anderson
Robert L. Drake
Robert Lansing
Robert Lynd
Robert Michael Ballantyne
Robert W. Chambers
Rosa Nouchette Carey
Rudyard Kipling
Saint Augustine
Samuel B. Allison
Samuel Hopkins Adams
Sarah Bernhardt
Sarah C. Hallowell
Selma Lagerlof
Sherwood Anderson
Sigmund Freud
Standish O'Grady
Stanley Weyman
Stella Benson
Stella M. Francis
Stephen Crane
Stewart Edward White
Stijn Streuvels
Swami Abhedananda
Swami Parmananda
T. S. Ackland

T. S. Arthur
The Princess Der Ling
Thomas A. Janvier
Thomas A Kempis
Thomas Anderton
Thomas Bailey Aldrich
Thomas Bulfinch
Thomas De Quincey
Thomas Dixon
Thomas H. Huxley
Thomas Hardy
Thomas More
Thornton W. Burgess
U. S. Grant
Upton Sinclair
Valentine Williams
Various Authors
Vaughan Kester
Victor Appleton
Victor G. Durham
Victoria Cross
Virginia Woolf
Wadsworth Camp
Walter Camp
Walter Scott
Washington Irving
Wilbur Lawton
Wilkie Collins
Willa Cather
Willard F. Baker
William Dean Howells
William le Queux
W. Makepeace Thackeray
William W. Walter
William Shakespeare
Winston Churchill
Yei Theodora Ozaki
Yogi Ramacharaka
Young E. Allison
Zane Grey

www.ingramcontent.com/pod-product-compliance
Lightning Source LLC
Chambersburg PA
CBHW031346170626
46807CB00002B/847